To the memories of my father, Zane Seidel, and my grandfather, Melvin Goldman. They introduced me to this game I love, and would have loved what Cal did.

Also, to my family, Nadine, Zach, and Kara. Thanks for your never-ending understanding and support on this one—it was needed badly and appreciated greatly.

CONTENTS

ACKNOWLEDGMENTS

The thing that fascinated me during the research and writing of this book was the fact that even now, five years after his retirement, people speak in such glowing terms about Cal Ripken Jr. The more I talked to people, the more I began to understand why. What Ripken did in his career—streak or no streak—represented so much that people loved. The bottom line was that Ripken just wanted to go to the ballpark and play every day. He wasn't like some of our egomaniacal stars today who desperately need attention all the time. He just wanted to play. Nothing more. Teammates, coaches, managers, fans, and acquaintances all spoke the same way. Nobody said even one bad word. It was amazing.

That's also what made this project so difficult. I didn't want this book to simply be a repeat of Ripken's career. That's been done. Sure, I talked about some of the great parts of his career. That has to be included, but I wanted this to be a little bit different. I talked about Ripken's work ethic, character, hitting ability, and moments to remember (in a unique way). People said a variety of very interesting things, which let the book take shape.

I also was fortunate to get a lot of help from a lot of different places. Ripken's PR guy has long been John Maroon, someone I've been lucky to know for several years. He gave me a great, long interview early on that helped give me real direction. While initially starting his new public relations firm, he took the time to talk to me and helped to gently guide me about some of the bigger events in Ripken's career.

John used to be the Orioles' PR director, and Bill Stetka was his assistant. I've also known Bill for many years, and he assisted me greatly. Stetka, now working Maroon's old job, and I had a long interview during an Orioles game last summer in which he laid out a number of scenarios and explained many stories that gave me a lot of ideas. Bill has always been a big help to me in a number of ways, and he did it again for this book. Thanks also to others in the Orioles PR department who answered questions when I had them.

Jay Moskowitz also helped in several different ways. The public relations and communications manager for Ripken Baseball, he did a lot of things that made putting this book together easier—and it would take too long to explain it. Thanks, Jay.

Thanks also to the Bowie Baysox, specifically PR director Ryan Roberts and marketing director Phil Wrye. Phil is a patient man as he's put up with me since 1998, and Ryan helped me get several interviews with those coaching and managing in the Eastern League who played with or knew Cal. That was a big plus for this and greatly appreciated.

A big thanks also to my editor at Sports Publishing LLC, Laura Podeschi. She came on late in the game and helped right the ship after some early stumbles. I greatly appreciated her patience, especially when I kept telling her I'd get something in by a certain time and would invariably screw it up. I also appreciated her understanding when I often had to change in mid-stream; something that let me get this book done in a fashion that I wanted. Laura, I don't know how you did it.

Thanks also to my good friend Stuart Zolotorow. We've worked together for over 13 years on various projects, and I've tried my best to drive him crazy. He has some beautiful pictures in this book and let me bounce a million ideas and complaints off of him. See, Stuart, I really did get the book done.

So many friends of mine in journalism helped in a way that I hadn't had in other projects. In my first two books, for some reason, I kept very close to the vest what I was doing, but I had to open up a bit on this one. Dave Ginsburg, who's covered everything major in the Maryland area for the Associated Press for many years and is a good friend, helped me in many ways. In addition to giving me a nice interview, he answered many little questions that allowed me to get details right. Much appreciated, Dave. *Frederick News-Post* sports editor Stan Goldberg has done the same thing for me. I always enjoy our lunches together at the Ravens games. The guidance of both was invaluable. Also, thanks to WBAL Radio's Keith Mills, a good friend of Cal's, for giving me lots of good information when we talked. Keep rolling, Keith.

Thanks also to my alma mater, UMBC, for putting in an "absolutely quiet" floor in the library I used to work at. That was a great help, especially on those occasional times when people followed the rules.

My family also was great during this. Nadine, Zach, and Kara understood all the time I had to spend on the project and were great in realizing what it was about. Every one of them did something at some point that helped me greatly. This meant the world to me, especially with all the things they've gone through in recent months.

I know my mom, Elaine Seidel, isn't a baseball fan. But we're working on it, and working hard. Keeping it in the family, congrats to my sister, Sara Jane Armuth, on finding a great guy in Lenny Armuth. I know he loves soccer—since he's a coach, he's got to—and I'm really sorry about what happened to the Mets last season. Well, sort of. My nephews, Matthew and Jeremy, should like this book, even though it's not about New York teams. But we're working on them, too.

Moving to my wife's side, in-laws Muriel and Leroy Handwerger also were great, answering questions and letting me run my mouth endlessly, as usual. My brand-new nephew, Maxwell, will hopefully be an Orioles fan. After all, he lives in Baltimore and his mom and dad, Lisa and Gary Jolbitado, understand the right way of things. It's an honor to be Max's godfather. My niece, Lily Handwerger, is already a beautiful piece of work, despite being only almost three. Her mom and dad, Shannon and Neil Handwerger, definitely understand the correctness in being Orioles' fans.

Thanks to friends who let me bite their ear off with ideas, complaints, and everything else. Andy and Devera Levin, Bruce and Nancy Craven, Mike Cramblitt, Donald Gordon, Neil Rubin, Stacy Karten, Randy Gartner, Howard Gartner, Dave Ginsburg, Stan Goldberg, Stan Rappaport, and any others I plum forgot. Also, thanks to Rich Scherr (as always), Sally and Seth Craven, Dan and Samantha Levin, Dan O'Connell (I owed you one!), Tom Matte, Don Morrison (in so many ways), and all the Harford County people who answered all my stupid questions.

Also, to the memories of my dad and grandfather, to whom I have dedicated this book. My dad took me to many baseball games, including a few in the World Series, before he died. We both loved the game and talked about it so much. I miss those days. My grandfather was kind enough to take me to games on a regular basis after my dad died, and he'll never know how much that meant to me as a confused and sometimes too-angry young kid. Sorry I can't send both of you a copy, but I'm sure you're looking down. If so, I'm sure you'll like it.

FOREWORD

I first met Calvin Edwin Ripken Jr. on March 1, 1975, the first day of baseball practice at Aberdeen High School that year. It was a cold, blustery day, with the remnants of a February snowstorm ringing the athletic fields at the school where Cal Ripken Sr. had begun his baseball journey a generation before. For young Calvin—no one called him Cal or Junior in those days—it was to be an inauspicious beginning for what was to follow. Asked to run a mile in six minutes, 30 seconds on that first day to prove they were in shape, most candidates for the team had little difficulty, but the 5-foot-6, 128-pound Calvin Ripken came up short. Convinced it would end his high school baseball career before it started, the plucky 14-year-old arranged to come in early the next morning and made the time with room to spare.

What followed was a storybook high school career in which Ripken, as a junior, led his team to its first county baseball championship in 19 years, and, as a senior, its first-ever state baseball title. Calvin Ripken Jr. was the kind of player a coach dreams of having just once in his career. The first on the field and the last off, he had a burning desire to improve—even when he became the best player in his league. Blessed with amazing hand-eye coordination, uncanny baseball instincts, and a rocket arm, he overcame his lack of foot speed with desire and anticipation.

Calvin Ripken was the ultimate teammate. Quiet but intense, he led by example and made losing a non-option. As later years and an unimaginable 2,632 consecutive-game major-league streak would confirm, his perseverance to be present for every inning of every game was a given.

This is a story of the local boy who went on to achieve greatness with his hometown team—a team coached and managed by his father and played on by his brother. This is a story of the small-town kid who rescued Major League Baseball from its strike-induced stupor by the strength of his character and his love of the game. This is a story so far-fetched that, had it not all been played out before our very eyes, none of us could have believed it possible.

—Donald R. Morrison

INTRODUCTION

B rooks Robinson has long been considered the most popular, or best known Oriole. So many fans remember his smiling face, his warm way with people, and his low-key personality that seemed to be a signature for the franchise—even though he wasn't the only reason the Orioles were arguably baseball's most consistent franchise from the mid-'60s to the mid-'80s.

But when Cal Ripken Jr. likely goes into the Hall of Fame this summer, he'll probably be the player that most baseball fans today will associate with the Orioles. Ripken and Robinson have an amazing number of similarities. Both are small-town guys with the accompanying polite mannerisms, and have never been too busy to talk with anybody. The two individuals are perfect examples of what has become the exception in professional sports in the 21st century.

After retiring, Robinson worked on the team's television broadcasts for several seasons and kept a known face in the community. Ripken behaved in a similar manner once his career ended following the 2001 season. After playing his entire career with the Orioles, the organization his father coached and managed with for so long, the Hall of Fame-bound shortstop/third baseman churned out a different path to success while remaining in the sport he loves and helping the town in which he grew up.

Ripken comes from the small town of Aberdeen in Harford County, about 35 miles north of Oriole Park at Camden Yards. When he retired, Ripken helped build up baseball in Maryland, going back to his hometown and constructing a new stadium, the first step in creating a baseball complex named after his father to honor the man's legacy as both a great teacher and coach.

The fact that Ripken built a baseball complex in Aberdeen and began the IronBirds, a very successful minor-league team that constantly sells out their games, impressed many in the area. Ripken is such a well known name that he could have done this anywhere, but he came back to his hometown, a fact that those in the area haven't forgotten. It's probably a big reason for his popularity since retirement.

Ripken's past portrays the classic hometown hero story. He grew up in the area, constantly came to Memorial Stadium, the former home of the Orioles, to work on his skills with his father. He took batting practice, fielding practice, and received help from players to improve his game. His hard work, even while a teenager and still in high school, is something that players like Doug DeCinces still remember 30 years later. DeCinces was the third baseman who took over for Robinson—and the player the Orioles traded when they gave that starting position to Ripken four years later.

People who've dealt with and know Ripken still talk fondly of him. Ernie Tyler, a man who has worked for the Orioles for over 46 years handing out balls to the umpires, remembers Ripken during his high school years. One of Tyler's sons played baseball against Ripken. Tyler still marvels at how Ripken's personality has never changed, how he'll look you right in the eye when shaking your hand—something that's the exception rather than the norm with celebrities.

It will be interesting to see the type of reaction Ripken gets when likely voted into the Hall of Fame this summer. How many Orioles fans will make the trek to Cooperstown to see Ripken's big day? Robinson earned so much popularity partially because some of his greatest moments were in huge games like the 1966 World Series, when he homered in his first at-bat to help the Orioles to a shocking four-game sweep of the Los Angeles Dodgers. And, as most Baltimore baseball fans know, the 1970 World Series belonged completely to Robinson as he made a number of spectacular defensive plays and had nine hits to lead the Orioles to a five-game victory over Cincinnati's "Big Red Machine."

While Robinson wound up in postseason play six times and came close several other times, Ripken didn't have nearly as many chances. The Orioles made postseason action only three times during Ripken's long career—and got to the World Series just once. Ripken made a memorable out in the 1983 World Series, catching a soft line drive to lock up Baltimore's five-game triumph, but he didn't get as much national notice until his run at Lou Gehrig's Iron Man streak took hold.

Ripken's timing arguably jolted Major League Baseball in the most positive way possible. He tied and broke Gehrig's record during the 1995 season, one year after a contentious labor dispute and strike wiped out much of the final two months of the season and the playoffs—including the World Series. But Ripken earned so much positive attention from his record, which touched so many people because of its simplicity. He was a man who earned worldwide publicity because he wanted nothing more than to keep coming to work on a daily basis, often with a team that wasn't terribly good.

But some fans were upset with Ripken and said he was more concerned with the streak than the team. However, as many have wondered, who else would have replaced him if he wanted a day off or two? Ripken's streak touched Baltimore fans as much as Robinson's 1970 World Series highlights. Ripken will have a huge number of fans at Cooperstown. It will be interesting to see just how many.

Where does Ripken go from here? He's looking at buying minor-league teams on a regular basis. The goal is to purchase 10 teams possibly over a 10-year period. Ripken bought a team in Augusta, Georgia, and also started his baseball academy in Myrtle Beach (South Carolina). He's quietly building his own baseball monopoly. The biggest question is how far he'll take it.

The whispers in the Baltimore area have grown louder in recent months that Ripken could put together a group to eventually purchase the Orioles from Peter Angelos. The Baltimore-based lawyer bought the team in 1993, but the Orioles have lost favor with their fans in the last several years after nine consecutive losing seasons. Attendance has dropped significantly at Oriole Park at Camden Yards, and Angelos has received a large amount of negative publicity.

This idea has been slowly gaining speed in Baltimore. *The Baltimore Sun* published an article discussing the situation in

September 2005. The article talked about how Ripken, "careful to speak in hypotheticals" due to his good relationship with Angelos, said, "I think I could have value to a group, an ownership group. I like Mr. Angelos, and I don't know what's going to happen to this club, but if it were for sale, it would be interesting to explore."

Angelos said that everyone wants to know if he will sell the club, but added that, "if such a day came, and [Ripken] was the person playing that role, I would say you couldn't find a better guy."

So, even though Ripken's playing days are long gone and he'll likely be in the Hall of Fame as one of the most memorable Orioles ever, he might become even more well known in the years to come. Ripken turned 46 late in the 2006 season, but it won't be surprising to see him continue his involvement in baseball. His well-known stature in the area and around the country will help him continue to be a big name in the sport.

1

HE WAS JUST CALVIN

D on Morrison is the public relations director for public schools in Harford County, Maryland, the county from which Cal Ripken Jr. comes. Ripken went to Aberdeen High School and played for the Eagles baseball team. Morrison coached him during his first three years there, and knows him well. When talking about Ripken today, Morrison unfailingly refers to him as "Calvin," rather than the well-known "Cal." It's just how he knows him.

The small-town-boy aspect of Ripken's life has been retold many times since he broke in with the Orioles late in the 1981 season. He was the hometown boy picked by the hometown team whose dad happened to be a manager in the Baltimore minor-league system, and was later a coach with the Orioles.

"I had heard through the grapevine that Cal Ripken Sr.'s son would be coming out for the team," Morrison said. "[He was supposed] to be a very good player, but his father was the name that was known. Cal's son was just that—his son. ... He was just Calvin. I had not met him."

Morrison had a good laugh over what happened the first day of baseball practice. Morrison had the boys run a mile and told them they needed to complete it in six and a half minutes or they wouldn't make the team.

"This little kid, who had a very high-pitched voice and was 5-foot-6 and 128 pounds—that was [Ripken's] height and weight in ninth grade—came to me and said he couldn't make the six minutes and 30 seconds," Morrison stated. "So I told him, 'Don't worry about it. You can come back tomorrow and try it again.' I told him we could break it down into half-mile segments, and that would be fine. The whole idea was that the kids knew they had to be in shape."

Morrison laughed at how determined the future Hall of Famer was, even then. "He came back the next day and made the 6:30—barely," Morrison said. "Running was never one of Calvin's favorite things." But Ripken loved working on his game so much that he truly was what Morrison calls a "diamond rat."

"Every summer, Vi [Cal's mother] would take the family and move to wherever Cal Sr. was and stay there the whole summer and come back just before school started," Morrison continued. "Calvin got major league instruction from people who were going to be all-stars. He enjoyed being the diamond rat. He idolized his father. He got to work with players like Doug DeCinces and Bobby Grich. He worked every day with those soon-to-be major league infielders."

Ripken had started strongly from the beginning of his career—even as a child. In an interview with the website *Junior Baseball*, Ripken mentioned that he didn't begin playing organized baseball until the age of eight. He said his team went 8-0 that summer. Ripken helped by playing pitcher and shortstop and batting .927. "I made one out the whole season," Ripken said.

He worked endlessly at learning the game, mastering the fundamentals, taking thousands of ground balls, and simply putting in extra time all the time. He didn't just want to practice. He wanted to practice perfectly. His Oriole teammates said later that this attitude probably helped him adjust to the big leagues that much faster and to become that much better.

In an article in *Outside Pitch* magazine, former Oriole second baseman Rich Dauer expressed the fact that Ripken wasn't just a new kid when joining the team. "When Cal got here," said Dauer, "he wasn't just around the Baltimore Orioles, he was around a lot of his own family. And he fit in perfectly. He played the game exactly the way the Orioles played it, which is to give it all to the team [without worrying] about what your stats or personal goals are. You play so the team will have the best chance to win every single time out on the field. He did that, and I think he's still doing it."

Ripken's work ethic certainly helped him learn how to play the game. Later on, Ripken and Oriole officials would face a dilemma as to whether he should be a pitcher or infielder. Interestingly, Morrison said that the Orioles were the only team that saw Ripken as a shortstop. Others took a look at the long, tall Ripken and said, "He's too slow—he's a pitcher."

Former Oriole Scott McGregor, one of the team's most reliable pitchers in the '70s and '80s and the winner of the final game of the 1983 World Series, had a quick answer when asked if he thought Ripken could have done well as a pitcher.

"Oh, yes," McGregor said with a smile. "No doubt about it. He could throw."

Morrison told Ripken that he'd be a shortstop and pitch once every three games at Aberdeen. He had no doubt then and has no doubt now. "We always saw him as an infielder because he had great hands and the technique to keep ... low," Morrison explained. "Whether he was born with it or learned it from the Orioles greats, he had it."

Morrison started Ripken as a freshman and initially put him at second base. He moved Ripken to shortstop later in the year when Ripken felt more comfortable going up against players who had a size advantage. He often batted eighth in the lineup because of his small size. But Morrison would sometimes move Ripken to the number-two spot because of his ability to lay down a bunt.

Ripken simply kept improving—and growing—throughout his high school career. "He ... became stronger, and he took his knowledge and his innate ability to become a great hitter," Morrison said. "He grew gradually, and by the time he was a junior, he was 6-foot-1, maybe 165 pounds. He continued growing after he graduated high school, adding about an inch a year until he was about 20 years old."

The baseball scouts took notice of Ripken and came to watch his games. His success was well documented at that time. He played in the Mickey Mantle World Series in Texas the summer after his junior season, and everything came together his senior year. Ripken hit .492 with 29 RBIs in 20 games. He did even better on the mound, posting a 7-2 record with a sparkling 0.70 ERA and 100 strikeouts in 60 innings.

Ripken played a huge role as Aberdeen won the Class A (now Class 3A) state title with a 7-2 victory in the championship game. The Orioles drafted him in the second round of the 1978 Amateur draft, and the rest, as they say, is history.

Cal Sr. rarely got to see his son play because of the Orioles' schedule, and his son understood and accepted that. But Vi Ripken was always there at both home and away games. Morrison said that she would sit in a low-slung chair right behind home plate and watch the action.

Morrison also said that when Ripken Sr. was around, he was very good about staying out of the way. He could have pushed, saying, "I'm a major-league coach, this is the way you should do it." But Morrison said the elder Ripken never did, which paid off for everyone. "His dad was away a lot, but Cal Sr. was very deferential, he never tried to interfere, never," Morrison said. "We were the [high school] coaches,

The Baltimore Orioles drafted Cal Ripken Jr. in 1978. The young athlete made his major-league debut on August 10, 1981. *(Photo by Stuart Zolotorow)*

and he was good about that. When Calvin was a freshman, and Cal Sr. was home because of the strike, they hadn't repaired the [school] fields yet because of the winter, and they were just horrible. Cal Sr. came to a practice, and [while] he was talking to us, took a look at the field and said, 'This is just terrible, I'll be right back.' I had no idea what he was doing. But he [showed up] with an old Plymouth Fury with the fins. He ... had an old chain-link drag that you used to drag fields with, and told [Cal's brothers] Billy and Fred to jump on and there they [went]. ... He must have gone around that field 25 times with Bill and Fred hanging on. By the time he was finished, that field looked like glass. If you think about Calvin, he got the good parts of both his mom and his dad. His dad was 'get it done, do it right.' His mom, much more soft, cares about everyone, just a caring individual. I think if you look at Calvin, you'll see a combination of 'get things done, no phony baloney about it, just get it right.'"

Morrison looks back on everything with amazement because, to him, Ripken hasn't changed at all nearly 30 years since graduating high school and becoming an internationally known celebrity. "He's just so kind to everyone," Morrison said.

Morrison remembered one moving occasion near the turn of the millennium when Aberdeen High dedicated Ripken Field, what they call their baseball field on the side of the school next to the football stands. It was a moment that showed how much a father meant to his son.

"Calvin gave a speech in which he was so emotional that he could barely speak," Morrison stated. "He motioned over to where the old field used to be and said that one of his fondest memories was seeing his father walking up over the hill to see him play high school ball. He always played his worst when his father was there. He just was so intent on showing his dad how good he was ... because his dad got to see him so seldom."

He Was Just Calvin

Ripken's quiet values have helped him remain in close touch with his hometown. Since retirement, Ripken has built a baseball complex in Aberdeen and has started a very successful minor-league team, the Aberdeen IronBirds. Ripken is now working to add more minor league teams to his portfolio, but everything started where he did—in Aberdeen, where he's still known as Calvin.

2

COMING TO THE MAJORS

C al Ripken Jr.'s major-league debut typified the sort of player he became—low-key but significant. The Orioles called him up from their top minor-league club, the Class AAA Rochester Red Wings of the International League, on August 10, 1981. An ongoing labor dispute between players and owners that had wiped out play for about two months was settled, and the games began again.

Ripken entered a deep, veteran-laden club that had challenged for the play-offs since Earl Weaver took over midway through the 1968 season. Weaver had joined the Orioles as a first-base coach and became manager during the All-Star break, while the Detroit Tigers ran away with the American League. Weaver did things his way. He tried everything and did not hesitate if he believed something would work. One of his first moves was to shift Don Buford to the outfield and place him in the leadoff spot. The change worked beautifully, and the Orioles won the American League pennant thrice between 1969 and 1971—and even captured a World Series title in 1970.

Breaking into the team's regular lineup was a difficult task. Solid players like Bobby Grich, Don Baylor, and Doug DeCinces had to wait longer periods for such a chance. But Ripken got his opportunity right away, going in as a pinch runner for outfielder Ken Singleton in the bottom of the 12th inning of a 2-2 tie with Kansas City.

Singleton started the 12th with a double to left off Renie Martin when Weaver put Ripken in to run. John Lowenstein followed with a single to right field, and Ripken raced around to score the winning run against a very good Kansas City team. First game and a winning run scored. Typical Cal.

Despite being brought up as a third baseman, Ripken was put in at shortstop at the end of Kansas City's 10-0 victory two days later. This was the first game in a doubleheader, and Ripken started the second game at third base, going 0-for-2 while batting seventh. But the veteran-filled team made getting good playing time difficult that season. Weaver put Ripken in during several situations, but the 21-year-old got only 39 at-bats. The 6-foot-4 Ripken finished with five hits and a .128 batting average as the Orioles battled for wins.

"He was surrounded by a lot of good guys," stated former Oriole McGregor. "We had a great team. Eddie [Murray] was there. Lowenstein was there. It was just a very good team. We were in the heat of the pennant race all the time. I think it's very important for a young guy when he comes up to the big leagues to have some good people around him. Everybody just encouraged him."

But the Orioles apparently saw something in Ripken and were confident enough to make a major move in the off-season. They traded starting third baseman DeCinces to the Angels for outfielder Dan Ford, which opened the door for Ripken. The Orioles knew Ripken a little better than most young players. They had seen him taking batting practice and working out with his father at Memorial Stadium—the team's home at that point.

"He came from a great lineage with Sr. as his dad," McGregor said. "Heck, he'd been around us. We'd all watch him come out and take batting practice three or four years in a row before he got drafted. ... He was familiar with all of us, so I think that helped."

Ripken takes batting practice prior to a game. After a rough start at the plate, he became a force in Baltimore's lineup. *(Photo by Stuart Zolotorow)*

Baseball's Iron Man: Cal Ripken Jr., A Tribute

The Ford trade created a spot in the starting lineup, and Ripken jumped right in, going 3-for-5 on opening day and showing some real pop in his bat. But he struggled badly after that, going just 4-for-52 the rest of the month, despite playing nearly every day. The criticism began. Were the Orioles rushing him simply because he was one of their coaches' sons? Was he not ready for the big leagues yet? After all, he was only 21.

But there was something about the kid that Weaver liked, and the skipper continued to put Ripken in the lineup every day, ignoring the growing calls to sit him down or send him back to the minors. Weaver wouldn't budge, even as Ripken's numbers kept slipping. By the end of April, Ripken was hitting a measly .123. He began May with an 0-for-3 effort against the Angels—the team he would break Gehrig's consecutive games mark against 13 ½ years later—and didn't seem to improve. The Orioles were trying to contend for the American League East championship once more, and Ripken's poor start had many worried. But a small incident helped turn things around.

Ripken had a talk with Angels slugger Reggie Jackson, a one-time Baltimore Oriole not shy about expressing his opinions. According to *Encyclopedia Britannica*, Jackson told the rookie to "do what Cal Ripken can do, not what others think you can do." In the same piece, Ripken said, "[My] father had been telling me that all along, but it didn't register. When Reggie said it, it sort of jolted something in there and brought me back to Earth."

Ripken's average had slid to an abysmal .117 after going 0-for-3 on May 1 versus the Angels, but Jackson's words proved helpful, and Ripken soon took off. He banged out six hits over three games against the Angels. Ripken then went on a tear, getting hits in 14 of 15 games. He had three homers in the month of May, and his batting average rose to a more respectable .245.

Coming to the Majors

Fans saw more of the same in June. Ripken hit .300 that month, raising his average to .267 overall with five homers and 21 RBIs, and seemed to settle into both the lineup and his everyday role.

Longtime Baltimore sportscaster Keith Mills believes there's no question how much Jackson's pep talk meant to the rookie. "I talked to Cal about that a lot," Mills said. "[Jackson] told him, 'Just do whatever you did that got you here. Just go up. Don't think—swing, hit, do what you have to do. Just be yourself. Relax and play the game the way you know how to play.' Also, Earl Weaver stuck with him. This day and age, I don't know if a manager would have done that. But Earl, he let him ride, and fortunately, Cal turned it around. Earl had this vision that he was going to be a big, power-hitting shortstop, which nobody else did. People wondered back then why they were moving him off third base. Because of his size, nobody thought he could handle it."

Although there was no doubt the youngster could play third, Weaver had indeed been contemplating the rookie's infield position. Many within the Oriole organization were critical of the change, because it went against the stereotype at that time. Shortstops were commonly shorter players with great range.

Ripken lacked good foot speed, so the experts didn't think he'd be able to cover the hole to the middle of the field. Nobody questioned his glove, but could he put himself in position to make some of the key plays a shortstop needs to take care of? Could he do it consistently?

The Orioles soon found out. Weaver had put Ripken at shortstop a few times since the rookie had come up the year before, but the manager finally made the move permanent on July 1.

"Earl had been talking about it quite a bit, and we knew it was going to happen sooner or later," McGregor said. "It was just whenever he decided to go ahead and do it—against everybody else's wishes—because nobody else wanted to. Cal took to it as a duck to water. And the rest was history after that. ...."

Pictured here in 1982, Ripken was named Rookie of the Year. *(Photo by Stuart Zolotorow)*

Coming to the Majors

Bill Ripken was still in high school during Cal's early years in the majors and didn't really understand the fuss. He knew his brother didn't have great foot speed, but he also knew there were plenty of other factors that went into playing shortstop.

"You know, Brooks Robinson was possibly one of the slowest ... [runners], but he had great anticipation and a great first step," Bill Ripken stated. "And Jr., being a student of the game, yes, he was smart, and yes, he knew where people were going to hit the ball ... but smartness will only get you so much. The fact that he was big [meant] he could reach out and catch the balls that some smaller guys couldn't get to."

Don Werner played parts of seven seasons in the big leagues and has managed in the Orioles' minor-league system throughout the opening years of the 21st century. Werner agrees with those who say that Ripken's success at shortstop has changed the way people view the position and has opened the door for bigger players like Derek Jeter and Alex Rodriguez.

"[Ripken] was just one of those guys that you just noticed because of his love of the game and his energy," Werner said. "That was back in the day when the shortstop ... was a short guy that was running all over the place and played great defense and hit .210 or .220. That was basically it at shortstop and at catcher. You didn't really care what the guys hit. Cal definitely showed it didn't matter what you looked like; it just mattered if you could move around and play the position," said Werner.

Ripken settled into the big leagues and his new position more as the season went on. As his offensive troubles went away, Ripken became a major contributor to the Baltimore lineup.

"He had those good instincts, and he had that good first step, and he had a great throwing arm," McGregor said. "He could be acrobatic and make throws from the hole. He just learned how to play."

The support of the Orioles' strong veteran group proved crucial to Ripken that season. Cal learned a lot from those who instructed him in his early days in Baltimore, specifically Gold Glove winner Mark Belanger, Baltimore's longtime shortstop, and Dauer, Ripken's double-play partner at second base during the first few years of his career. Both players taught Ripken the right way to do the job. He absorbed this knowledge and became that much better a player.

"They had so many veteran guys on that team," Mills said. "Eddie [Murray] was big with him. Eddie was huge. Like Reggie, he supported him through good times and bad. I think because those guys were always in his corner that even when he struggled, he said, 'You know what? I must be good enough to play at this level, because these guys are telling me I'm good enough … just go out and play.' I think that's what happened. He just went out and started playing."

He began playing well, going from a rookie whose abilities many questioned to a major part of the Baltimore roster. Ripken fit into an Oriole lineup that was one of the American League's strong attacks. They had four players hit at least 20 homers, led by first baseman Murray's 32 homers and 110 RBIs. Ripken came next with 28 homers and 93 RBIs, followed by outfielders John Lowenstein (24 homers, 66 RBIs) and Gary Roenicke (21 homers, 74 RBIs). Ripken often batted third or fifth and helped the Orioles on a late run.

Baltimore sat 7½ games out after an August 19 loss at Minnesota. Manager Harvey Kuenn's Milwaukee Brewers—nicknamed Harvey's Wallbangers because of their prodigious power—were banging out homers and scoring runs at an alarming rate while beating just about everyone. But the Orioles finally began to rally in late August, winning 17 of 18 and pulling to three games back in early September. Ripken continued to play a major role.

The Orioles were also sparked emotionally by Weaver's somewhat surprising announcement that he would retire at the season's end. They wanted to win one more for their tough skipper, who had led them to so many victories. Baltimore nearly pulled it off, still sitting three games out with four games left, when Milwaukee came to town for a season-ending, four-game series.

In a historical weekend in Baltimore, the Orioles swept the Friday night doubleheader and won again on Saturday afternoon to tie the Brewers and send the town into madness. With Jim Palmer scheduled to pitch against fellow veteran Don Sutton, the fans were sure the team could pull off a victory on Sunday. Palmer's record in big games was impressive and lengthy, but the Brewers took the game. Robin Yount homered in the top of the first, sending Milwaukee on its way to a 10-2 victory.

Ripken only had two hits in the series. But one was a two-run homer—his final long ball of the season. He had certainly cemented his place with the Orioles. The shortstop was voted Rookie of the Year, a feat that was even more impressive, considering how badly he'd played in the first few weeks.

"The one thing I've always marveled about him is the mental toughness that he had," Mills said of Ripken. "Even later, when we played basketball together, he would show this sign of competitiveness in a very restrained way that made you say, 'Now I know why he had that success at the major league level.' He could handle adversity, and he could handle success the same way. Never changed his demeanor. Never changed his personality. Never changed his outlook."

3

MVP, YEAR TWO

The Orioles were looking for Ripken to play a big part on their 1983 team. New manager Joe Altobelli was familiar to many of the Birds, having been a manager with the team's Class AAA affiliate at Rochester for several years. A different skipper from Weaver, Altobelli was more low-key and quiet—a welcomed change to some. Altobelli was fortunate to take over a well-stocked veteran team ready for a shot at postseason play. The players were completely familiar and comfortable with their roles.

The more relaxed Altobelli understood how to handle an experienced team. McGregor laughed when describing one particular incident. Weaver had worked hard rotating outfielders like Roenicke, Lowenstein, and Benny Ayala into the lineup, giving the Orioles strong play in left field and even at designated hitter. Altobelli kept that system going and once, before he had even called out the switch, both players involved had already changed things up themselves.

Ripken fit nicely into the team because, despite being only 22 when the season began, he had the savvy and presence of a veteran player. This probably resulted from being raised in a baseball family, often on a baseball field, and understanding so much about the game. Officially, Ripken was just in his second full year in the majors, but he played like someone much older. The Orioles knew and appreciated this, especially when he continued to blossom in 1983.

Ripken also had much less pressure put on him. He had already proven his ability to play at the major league level by winning the Rookie of the Year award and helping the Orioles rally from far back before losing the American League East title by just one game. The Orioles were comfortable with Ripken at shortstop—a move people were now lauding.

Ripken followed two great Orioles shortstops. Luis Aparicio played a key role on the Orioles' first championship team in 1966. Mark Belanger, despite battling hitting problems throughout his career, held the job for over a decade with a true style people still remember to this day. The long and lean shortstop was magical with balls to the hole and could seemingly make any play. Ripken performed differently, using guile and gumption and brains to make everything look routine.

"Cal was a rock in 1983, coming after Mark Belanger," Mills said. "I thought no one could come close to Belanger at shortstop. Even though Cal didn't make the spectacular plays like Belanger did, he was just as steady. He made every routine play that was hit to him. I never saw Cal blow the double-play ball. I think that having that consistency out there, for him to go out there and be consistent from day one, Joe Altobelli didn't have to worry about the shortstop."

Ripken loved his job and wanted to do everything he could to enjoy where he was in life. McGregor said that Ripken still acted like a kid. "He was just fun, life was a game to him," McGregor revealed. "Every time we came into the clubhouse, he was playing stickball and that kind of stuff. I lockered next to him. ... He was always bugging me about [the fact that] ... my cleats were on his side of the locker, and I came in one day, and he had a piece of tape going from the top of the locker to out on the floor. He said, 'This is my side, this is your side, keep your stuff off [my side].' I said, 'Get a life.'"

The group also accepted Ripken. "… That was one thing that was neat about the team, nobody ever had that air about them that they were, like, the leader. He just became part of the group, and that's what made us good," said McGregor. A veteran-filled team could have made it difficult for the youngster, but many of them were coached by his father and had known Ripken since he was a child. Plus, the ballplayer's talent spoke volumes. Ripken wasn't the type of ballplayer that many try to be today. He lacked flash and glitz, but worked hard to make the plays that individuals are supposed to make on a regular basis.

How solid was Ripken that season? He became the first player to ever play every inning in every game from the regular season to the playoffs all the way through the World Series. He also became the first player to win the Rookie of the Year trophy and Most Valuable Player award in consecutive years.

Frustration had been mounting in Baltimore since the 1979 season, when the Orioles blew a three games-to-one lead in the World Series and watched the Pittsburgh Pirates rally to win the final three games to take the championship. Many baseball experts had already given the Orioles the title when they scored a wild come-from-behind victory in Game 4.

Weaver had gambled a bit in Game 5, starting Cy Young Award winner Mike Flanagan on three days' rest. Flanagan threw well for six innings, but Pittsburgh broke the game open against the bullpen in a 7-1 victory.

Although the final two games were in Baltimore, the usually powerful Oriole lineup scored just one run in both outings. The Pirates beat Palmer 4-0 in Game 6 to tie the Series at three games apiece. McGregor threw well in Game 7, but Pittsburgh pulled out a 4-1 victory to win the championship.

The Orioles made no secret as to what they desired when clinching a spot in the 1983 playoffs. They had come so close in the past and wanted to come away with a World Series title this time.

Ripken played a big role in the American League Championship Series against the Chicago White Sox. The Orioles won that best-of-five series in four games, but it wasn't easy. Chicago's LaMarr Hoyt shut down the Orioles for a 2-1 victory in Game 1 in Baltimore. Ripken got the Orioles' lone RBI, a ninth-inning single, but Murray grounded into a force play to end the game.

But the Orioles rebounded for a 4-0 victory in Game 2 as rookie surprise Mike Boddicker, going the distance to tie the series, continued his great season with an amazing 14-strikeout three-hitter. Ripken also came up big, doubling and scoring in a two-run sixth inning to help the Orioles break things open. Baltimore then took command when the series shifted back to Chicago for Games 3 and 4.

The Orioles started quickly in Game 3 when Murray blasted a three-run homer off Richard Dotson in the first inning en route to an 11-1 victory. Murray had called out Chicago manager Tony La Russa after a close pitch, and the team's quiet leader seemingly awoke, which appeared to spark the Orioles. Baltimore then pulled out a dramatic 3-0 victory over the White Sox the following afternoon to win their first American League championship in four years.

Baltimore then went on to beat the Philadelphia Phillies in the World Series, four games to one. The Orioles, despite being an experienced ball club, had problems in the series. Philadelphia took the first game in Baltimore, and the Orioles took Game 2. Ripken's RBI single gave the Orioles their final run in a 4-1 decision. The Orioles then had to rally for a come-from-behind victory against Hall of Famer Steve Carlton in Game 3. Ford played a big role in the game, a 3-2 victory. Another Hall of Famer, Palmer, earned his last major league win in the same game, coming on to pitch two innings of relief after Flanagan struggled through the first four innings. Palmer was still

Ripken congratulates Eddie Murray as he crosses home plate during the 1983 World Series.
(Photo by Focus on Sport/Getty Images)

the pitcher on record when the Orioles put together two runs in the seventh inning to win the game. Probably the greatest pitcher in Orioles history, he would retire early in 1984.

Ripken helped in an early two-run rally in Game 4 the next afternoon, leading the Orioles to a tough 5-4 victory. "In 1983, when we got up three games to one, you could have heard a pin drop in the clubhouse," McGregor explained. "We said we're going to win the next one this time. But you have to be able to eliminate all those pressures and find a place where you just go out and make it feel like you're playing Little League ball again."

This time Baltimore wouldn't let go. McGregor went the distance, and the Orioles hit three home runs en route to a 5-0 victory to clinch the title. Murray broke out of his slump with two monstrous homers, the second of which was a two-run shot scoring Ripken, who had just walked.

Ripken recorded the biggest out of the series. With two outs in the bottom of the ninth, Garry Maddox swung at a McGregor pitch and lofted a soft line drive that Ripken caught with no trouble. Ripken held the ball in his glove and shook it with glee as the celebration began on the Veterans Stadium infield. The Orioles had finally won it all.

"[Ripken] was right there," McGregor said. "One thing good about Cal, he was nice and tall out there, and he'd catch a lot of those little liners that some people didn't catch. That was a great culmination for him, obviously the first year in 1982 being Rookie of the Year and then being voted the Most Valuable Player—of course, he didn't know it at the time—and then to get to a World Series and to win [it]. I know at that time we all thought, 'Heck, you're going to be doing this for a while with this team' … little did you know that was the only time he'd ever get there. It was a very special time."

Dempsey went 5-for-13 with some very clutch hits to win the World Series Most Valuable Player Award. Dempsey said that if it weren't for players like Ripken doing their jobs the way they did, he'd never have gotten a chance at the award.

Dempsey said Ripken might have been the final piece of the puzzle for the Orioles. "Pitching was always first, and we protected our pitching with great defense, and alongside of that great defense, which filters down to your offense, we had enough guys in the lineup to hit the ball out of the ballpark," said Dempsey. "Earl wanted that sort of offensive ballclub, and we could put some runs up on the board. There was no other team in baseball at that time that could compare to our team from a power standpoint with Eddie Murray, a switch-hitter, Ken Singleton, a switch-hitter, good power. Guys like Roenicke and Lowenstein doing the job they did … and then Cal coming along and being the player he was. We had all the pieces put together back then."

Ripken edged Murray for the American League's Most Valuable Player award, although the final numbers were good for both players.

Murray finished with a team-high 33 homers and also led the Orioles with 111 RBIs. He batted .306 with 178 hits and 115 runs scored. Ripken's numbers were right there, however, as he finished with a .318 batting average and 27 homers to go along with 102 RBIs. He also banged out 47 doubles as part of his 211 hits and scored 121 runs, barely edging Murray in the voting.

Some thought that Murray should have won the award, and others wondered about the effect of his cool relationship with the media. Murray didn't talk much with reporters as time went on. By 1986, he flat-out would not speak with the Baltimore media after being criticized by then-team owner Edward Bennett Williams in a local paper. His anger toward the press has persisted ever since. Ripken, however, was a different case. He didn't have much trouble dealing with the media, who loved his hometown-boy story.

McGregor said Ripken actually might have had too much good attention at times. "When he first became famous, he'd come in all the time and be worn out from doing all these appearances and stuff, and I said, 'The biggest word you're going to have to learn is "no," ... because you can't go out there and wear yourself out. I know you're a home-grown boy and everybody knows you and you're having a great time, but you have to balance all that stuff out.' He was always very conscious about that, always very aware of who he was and very proud of Aberdeen, his dad, and his reputation, and he took care of that. But at the same time, at the ballpark, he was just a kid in the uniform and he had a blast."

Bill Ripken said he often compared his brother's career to that of Dan Marino, a football player for the Miami Dolphins. "He and Marino, they were both life-long with one team," Bill Ripken said. Both did so much so early in their playing days. Marino was part of the fabulous quarterback draft of 1983, quickly became the Miami starter, and then led the Dolphins to the Super Bowl one year later. San Francisco routed the Dolphins in that game and many people said that Marino shouldn't worry because he'd have plenty more chances. But despite coming close several times, he never made it back, nor did Ripken ever win another World Series.

4

THE DIFFICULT YEARS

R ipken had already hit his stride and had become well known by the 1986 season. It was the team's first full year under Weaver—the second time around—and Baltimore was trying to rebound after disappointing seasons in 1984 and 1985. Team owner Edward Bennett Williams brought in Joe Altobelli after Weaver stepped down following the 1982 season, and the former Rochester Red Wings manager's modest approach proved successful as the Orioles won the World Series in his first season.

Altobelli loved Ripken's simple approach to his job. He just wanted to play as much as possible. Every inning of every game? Sure, no sweat. He'd do it and keep doing it as long as he could. It was something Altobelli talked about with *The Sporting News* as Ripken neared Gehrig's record in 1995.

"One time I asked him, 'What makes you want to play every inning of every game?' He told me when he first came up 1981, he sat the bench. And he promised himself if he ever got in the lineup, he wouldn't beg out," said Altobelli. "He stuck to his guns."

But everything began to fall apart after Altobelli's first year as manager. Although the Orioles had most of their key players like Ripken return for the following year, they were aging fast. Other teams also were catching up. The Orioles lived for years off a good minor-league system that churned out star player after star player at an amazing rate. Individuals like Ripken, Murray, Boddicker, Scott McGregor, John Shelby, and many more with a role in the championship all spent some time in the Oriole farm system.

The well, however, was starting to run dry. Williams, like George Steinbrenner and so many others in baseball, fell in love with free agency. It was a fairly new concept in baseball, but the game was changing fast. Williams began trying to sign five-star, marquee names, but, as with so many other teams, bringing in high-priced superstars wasn't always a perfect fit. A lot of the players commanding large salaries had something else in common—they were either on the downside of their careers or were about to begin that long, slow slide.

The Orioles were starting to slide themselves, and Altobelli didn't make it past the first part of the 1985 season. Weaver returned, but found he didn't quite enjoy it as much as the first time around. Things had changed a lot in a short amount of time. He announced that he'd step down for good after the 1986 campaign, and the elder Ripken got the job.

But the timing wasn't good. The Orioles were falling apart. The 1987 team finished with a 67-95 record and placed sixth in the American League East. This surprised a number of people, since the 1986 team was in the fight for the division title until the last six weeks of the season. But despite an 11-game winning streak out of the All-Star break, nothing went right. The team struggled, but they were hopeful for better things in 1988. However, it only got worse—and very fast.

The 1988 season was a disaster from the start. Milwaukee swept a two-game series in Baltimore, and Cleveland then crushed the Orioles in a four-game set on the road. Management made a shocking decision that they knew would have reverberations. They fired Ripken Sr. after

As second baseman, Billy Ripken (3) joins his brother in the field.
(Photo by Jonathan Daniel/Getty Images)

just six games. It was difficult enough for people to swallow, but became even harder since the departed skipper's son was a top player.

The Orioles made the change quickly, a move that surprised many despite the problems the team was having at the start. Moves are rarely made so early in the season. There was no question that the Orioles simply were not a good team that season. They quickly went on to become a national joke, losing their first 21 games of the year before finally beating the White Sox in Chicago. But everyone agreed that blaming the elder Ripken and taking his job made little sense.

Ripken's brother, Bill, had made it to the Orioles by this point to become Cal's double-play partner. Bill Ripken had previously worn No. 3 as a second baseman. But after the Orioles fired his father, he changed it to No. 7 as an obvious show of support.

"Obviously, I was hurt by the whole thing," said Bill Ripken. "I just looked at Dad as being No. 7. I really didn't want anything going on during the course of the year, and it just occurred to me that somebody else could be given No. 7, and I just didn't like that thought very much. I just couldn't bear to think about it at that time."

Cal Ripken Jr. had started to emerge as a team leader around this time. He was truly becoming one of the game's most dominant players. The streak had slowly started to evolve, and people were beginning to mention it. Miss a game? Hell, Ripken hadn't even missed an inning in about five years. He just kept on playing through all the madness. It was a time of transition for a franchise that had been a model of efficiency in Major League Baseball for over two decades. But everything was crumbling down.

The Orioles also faced the possibility of losing Ripken. The firing of his father, the true mentor and teacher in his life, angered him for obvious reasons. Could the Orioles have lost him to free agency? Possibly, or if this had happened several years later, Ripken could have demanded a trade, as many players love to do today. But Ripken didn't do that. He simply gritted his teeth and worked through the situation.

The Difficult Years

Ted Patterson is a longtime Baltimore radio and TV reporter and author who covered the Orioles before, during, and after Ripken played for the team. He said that these times appeared difficult for Ripken, but his hard work and ability to focus on the task at hand—for him, getting to the park every day and just doing his thing—kept him moving along.

"Just his overall work ethic was what [was good]," Patterson said. "No matter what the team was doing, he was going to make sure he was ready to go and solid. He was already taking some heat then for the streak, but he muddled through all of that. He's a guy that just, as he said it, went to work every day and no matter what the standings showed, he was going to give it his best shot. Obviously he was not happy. But he still stuck on with the Orioles. He's not a guy that's very demonstrative, as far as his emotions, I thought maybe there was going to be a parting of the [ways] around that time. But he suddenly maybe cooled off a little bit and realized they had to make a move, even though Frank Robinson came on board and the same thing just continued on, the losing streak. That made 1989 all the better, I guess."

The 1989 Orioles were one of the biggest surprises of all time in baseball. Most thought that the Orioles would continue to provide baseball fans with many more laughs. And why wouldn't they assume that? The Orioles finished with a 54-107 record, couldn't get any pitcher—a starter or otherwise—to win 10 games, and were loaded with unproven younger players and older guys trying to hang on, along with new players trying to break through. It made for an unpleasant mix.

In fact, the pitching staff had most people scratching their heads and made infielders like Ripken terribly busy. The only pitcher who had a winning record was reliever/spot starter Dave Schmidt. He went 8-5 with a save in the historic win over Chicago, ending the nightmarish 21-game losing streak at the start of 1988.

But some subtle changes improved things in 1989. The pitching staff began to fare better under Robinson. Baltimore traded longtime starter Boddicker to Boston as part of the Brady Anderson trade, a deal that would keep the speedy outfielder in Baltimore for over a decade and brought Ripken a close friend. Even though Anderson struggled at the plate and batted only .207, he proved to be a solid defensive outfielder that, when in the game, helped the Orioles.

The Boddicker trade meant the Orioles needed even more help from their starting staff. Jeff Ballard had a career year in 1989. He went 18-8, and said many times how much the team's defensive strength—especially in the outfield—helped him. Rookie starter Bob Milacki also had a career year. The bulldog-like right-hander posted a 14-12 record, and gave the Orioles a strong pair of starting pitchers. Schmidt came back with a 10-13 record and, even though he struggled at times, pitched well enough to give the Orioles three starters with at least 10 victories—a vast improvement over the previous season, in which they had none.

The Orioles also suddenly got a lot of help from their bullpen. Much like Schmidt, Mark Williamson had been a spot starter and reliever in 1988. He'd been effective at times, but the Orioles made the tall right-hander a full-time middle and set-up guy in 1989. Williamson also had a career year, finishing 10-5 with a 2.93 ERA in 65 appearances. He became a solid reliever who helped back up the starters and paved the way to the season's biggest pleasant surprise—rookie Gregg Olson.

Baltimore picked Olson first in the 1988 amateur draft after his stellar career in college. The Orioles had high hopes for Olson, who joined the team late in the 1988 season with a 1-1 record in 10 games. But they handed him the closer's job in 1989, and the American League wasn't ready for his jaw-dropping, backbreaking curve ball. The combination of starting pitching and a strong, young back end of the bullpen changed everything.

The Difficult Years

Suddenly, the joke was on the rest of the American League. "They were a team, like the Tigers of 2006, that nobody gave any hope to," Patterson said. "They had everything kind of jell. Frank was suddenly not quite manager of the year, but close. It was definitely a transition time as some of the young guys ... were coming up, well, a lot of things started to happen. But Cal was the rock, the guy that was going to be there every day. They felt they had to live up to his standards and try to emulate him as best they could. His standard was one of excellence and total commitment and go about your business and not make waves and be a big leaguer."

Ripken played a big role in the way the success of 1989 began. The Orioles opened their season on a very cold afternoon against Boston at Memorial Stadium. The Red Sox threw 25-year-old starter Roger Clemens, who was rapidly rising as one of baseball's best pitchers. No one even realized then he'd be around for about 17 more years. Boston had won the American League East the previous year before Oakland rolled to a victory in the Championship Series, but the Red Sox appeared loaded again. For this reason, many didn't think the Orioles would get off to a very good start.

But Ripken blasted a three-run homer off Clemens to left field, helping the Orioles pull out a 5-4 victory. There would be no losing streak this year, and those involved with the team said that single hit truly set the stage for a good season.

"It made the win more sweet," then-manager Frank Robinson said to *The Baltimore Sun*, "and it might have set the tone for the year, going out and battling, not giving up."

Actually, Ripken's homer didn't even win the game. Boston had a 3-1 lead when Ripken struck. Boston then scratched out a run in the seventh to force extra innings, and the Orioles later won the game on Craig Worthingon's RBI single in the 11th. But talk to most anybody who had anything to do with the Orioles, and they'll tell you that Ripken's hit was big in so many ways. It told the Orioles they could

During better times, father and son converse in the Orioles dugout.
(Photo by Rich Pilling/MLB Photos via Getty Images)

come back against one of the game's best right-handers. On a very young team, this was a very big message.

"I think he was an influence by example," said Stan Goldberg, sports editor for the *Frederick News-Post*. "I didn't see him as a vocal leader, but I think that people looked up to him. I think the fact that he stuck that out from 1988 after his father was fired and didn't complain as much as he could have [helped]. He complained but he didn't go overboard, and I think that might have helped him the next year when people realized [if] he could be this way and stick with this team after what happened to him and his father, then they could do that too."

Goldberg said the fact that Ripken was able to keep going in such a professional manner sent a loud message. Everyone would have their own way of dealing with something like that—which is why Bill Ripken changed his jersey number—but still playing hard after his father was fired sent a strong message, especially to a very young team searching for its way.

"It's a good example of someone who was so much of a team player that it impressed the other young people," Goldberg said. "I think this was tremendously difficult for him in 1988 because if you remember, everyone was playing this up. It was a huge national story. The big thing was he played for his father. This thing was huge and then to have his father get fired six games into the season I think had a tremendous effect on him, and I think in today's age, most players would quit and say I don't care and leave, and the fact that he didn't do that showed me something. And they came back to his father and honored his father. At the time, his father was the scapegoat. The son was upset but did not react in a negative way. Frank lost the last 15 of those games at the start of 1988, and I'm sure that hurt too, because how could [they blame his] father when no one [could] win with this team?"

Getting through that period proved crucial to Ripken's stay in Baltimore. The team fared better over most of the next six or seven years, contended for the division title, and made the playoffs in 1996 and 1997. None of it, however, would have happened if Ripken hadn't been able to make his way through those few difficult years. After that bad stretch, the streak had become a reality, Ripken became the player that most identified as the main Oriole, and everything was lined up for the second half of Ripken's career.

5

THE STRIKE AND THE STREAK

The strike that ended the 1994 season in August nearly gave the sport a black eye from which it might have never recovered if not for Ripken and the Streak. The strike was a typical sports labor dispute—an ugly battle between two sides, neither of which would budge. The strike wiped out most of the final two months of 1994, surprisingly eliminating the playoffs and World Series and infuriating fans.

Baseball has been a staple of American summers since the 1800s. Boys begin playing the game when they are very little and never stop. They sleep with gloves underneath their pillows, fall in love with their hometown teams, and follow every move the players make. But the problems in 1994 were bad ones. The owners were alarmed at the game's financial situation and wanted a salary cap to put a lid on spending.

The players steadfastly refused to agree to this and walked out on August 12. Both sides talked, battled, and fought before the postseason was called off 32 days later—the first time any sport had lost its playoffs and championship to labor problems. The strike actually lasted 234 days into the next spring, ending when a federal judge issued an injunction versus the owners, and 1995 started under the previous contract's conditions.

But this was the eighth work stoppage in baseball history, and became the ugliest in many ways. The fact that the strike couldn't be solved in the summer, the fall, or even over the winter and looked like it would wipe out some or all of the 1995 season proved distasteful to many fans. Replacement players were ready to go, and some had already crossed the picket line during the short spring training of 1995. The shortened season didn't begin until late April, when baseball worked hard to remove itself from under a black cloud. This is one reason why Ripken's pursuit of Gehrig's consecutive games played record became so popular during 1995.

Gehrig's record was one that many in baseball thought was unbreakable, and his streak ended in a dramatic and sad fashion. Gehrig had performed with good numbers throughout 1938. He had 29 homers and 114 RBIs with a .295 batting average—not bad for a 36-year-old who hadn't missed any games in what seemed like a lifetime. But something was clearly off in 1939, when Gehrig went just 4-for-28 at the start of the season. Showing the class that had been his trademark throughout his career, Gehrig stopped the streak on May 2, fearing it was hurting the team to have him in the lineup.

It was discovered just a few weeks later that Gehrig had been suffering from amyotrophic lateral sclerosis, a fatal and crippling illness. He died two years later, and his illness thereafter became known as Lou Gehrig's disease.

As the 1995 season went on, Ripken began fielding more comparisons of himself to Gehrig, which he downplayed. He never wavered with regard to the Streak—Ripken continually saw himself as a man just doing his job.

Ripken's story represented something different in baseball—the idea of unselfishness. It gave fans a story about a man who wanted nothing more than to come to work every day and do his duty. It

Prior to a June 1990 game, Ripken leans against the Lou Gehrig memorial monument at Yankee Stadium. *(Photo by Ronald C. Modra/Sports Imagery/Getty Images)*

seemed rather simplistic, but it meant something huge for the game and the sport.

"Baseball really needed a feel-good moment, and that was it," said Dave Ginsburg, an Associated Press sportswriter who covers the Baltimore ballclub. "People were still a little bit sour from the strike. This was just someone who loved the game of baseball and wanted to play."

John Maroon joined the Orioles that year to take charge of the team's media relations and later went on to handle Ripken's public and media relations as a full-time job. Maroon said that the Orioles actually knew media interest in Ripken would be heavy, so he had to balance the amount of coverage and keep the shortstop away from the crush whenever possible.

Maroon also agreed that Ripken's race toward Gehrig's record and baseball's attempt to recover from the strike actually turned out to be an unusual match that helped both sides. So many regular fans were angry at baseball. People who earned regular, everyday salaries found it hard to sympathize with the players, but Ripken seemed to be someone with whom most fans could identify.

"I think it played a big role, because I think people were down on the game," Maroon stated. "They were sick of it, and they were looking for something a little more pure. The reason that Cal resonates with so many people I think is because it was all about showing up. He gets tons of letters from people that haven't missed a day of work or kids that have set attendance marks. It was something that the everyday person could relate to. Showing up is half the battle. I think the strike definitely made it larger than it was."

So Maroon said he expanded on an idea that he saw Texas Rangers PR director John Blake use during Nolan Ryan's last year in baseball. During the first game of each road series, the media interviewed Ryan. When the Orioles traveled, Maroon made Ripken available to the area's media on the first day to talk about the Streak, but that was all on the subject for the rest of the team's stay.

"I think Cal really appreciated the fact that every single day wasn't inundated with streak questions and inquiries," Maroon said. "He had a little peace built in. Everyone who knows Cal even a little knows he's very meticulous and he's a planning guy. He's not big on surprises, hates surprises. The more things are planned out for him, the more comfortable he is. And so this plan [of how to deal with the media regarding the Streak] that I presented to him he loved right away. He loved the concept of it. Because it was structure. He needs structure. He's such a schedule guy."

Ripken changed each of the scheduled press gaggles in a way that typified him.

The Strike and the Streak

"He was very self-conscious about it not affecting his teammates," said Maroon. "He asked, 'Can we do it several hours before everyone arrives?' They'd do a 1 or 2 p.m. thing before a night game. The PR directors for each of the teams would really help get the word out. He'd sit there for an hour. He'd take every question, and he'd do a couple of one-on-ones. That allowed him to not think [about the] Streak for a couple of days and decompress. It gave the press everything they needed and got it to them in a timely fashion."

Maroon explained that he asked all the Baltimore-area reporters how often they wanted to talk to Ripken. They said once a month would work, so that's how often they met with him. But requests came from everywhere, and the demands upon the Orioles, the PR staff, and Ripken grew as more outlets wanted one-on-one time. The country seemed to latch onto the Streak and constantly wanted more information as Ripken neared the record.

"As you might imagine, with September 5 and 6, at first we weren't sure how big they were going to be," Maroon said. "But as the season began to climb and as the team began to fall … it was all about Cal and the Streak. We realized this was going to be a huge event."

Maroon said it turned out to be as big as a playoff or World Series game. The only difference was that he and Bill Stetka, the pair who guided the media relations office, and their assistants had to run the monstrous task on their own. If it were a playoff game, Major League Baseball would have been there to help. But the Orioles were very helpful in working with them to accommodate the press. The team let the media take sections of seats in the outfield and turn them into an auxiliary press box. Maroon said the Orioles actually gave out media credentials to over 100 members of the media from outside the United States, and he thinks they issued over 1,000 credentials overall.

"I still think there were parts of that whole season that were tough for [Ripken] to take because it wasn't him," Baltimore sportscaster Keith Mills, a longtime friend of Ripken, said. "It was not his personality to be elevated above everybody else. Even though that's why he played the game—because he wanted to be the best—he didn't want to be in the spotlight."

Ripken did one thing that kept him in a bit of a limited spotlight in the final part of the season. He would quietly walk out and sign autographs for fans after the games.

"It was literally [for] hours after the game," Ginsburg said of each autographing session. "He thought it was the type of thing that the fans liked. It was to give something back to the fans. I think he thought the fans, and rightfully so, got more of a kick out of it than he did. He didn't just slap a Cal Ripken Jr. on [something]. He took pride in making sure it was lengthy. He had something to say to everyone."

"He loved the fans," Mills said. "He liked interacting with the people. As his career went on, I think it wore on him to have to deal with all the things he had to deal with every day—that's a personal opinion. All he wanted to do was play. [The Streak] became this mountain of a thing that everyone had to deal with. Is Cal going to play today? Where's he staying? Who's he going home with? To me, that was absurd scrutiny that didn't need to be done."

It didn't help that the Orioles were struggling that season. During the strike, the team had hired Phil Regan as its manager for the 1995 season after dismissing Johnny Oates, who reportedly did not always see eye-to-eye with owner Peter Angelos. Regan had been best known for his success with the Dodgers during the 1966 season when he made the All-Star team with an impressive 14-1 record as a relief pitcher for the National League champions. In an interesting twist, the Dodgers played the Orioles in the 1966 World Series, and Baltimore shocked everyone by sweeping Los Angeles in four straight games.

Many expected the Orioles to hire Davey Johnson that season. Johnson had played for the team during its incredibly successful streak, which included four World Series appearances in six years. The

The Strike and the Streak

Orioles won the 1966 Series, and made it back for three straight years between 1969 and 1971. Johnson started as the second baseman on all four World Series teams and later became a very successful major-league manager. He guided the New York Mets to a World Series title in 1986 and later managed the Reds to a division title. Cincinnati was on track for another when the strike hit in 1994. So Johnson stayed with the Reds, and the Orioles hired Regan instead.

At 58 years old, Regan had never before managed a game in the major leagues. He didn't really connect with some of the younger players, and the Orioles, who had been contenders for the American League East crown in 1994, never truly competed. The team was a major disappointment and didn't fare any better than one game over the .500 mark.

For this reason, a major part of any news regarding the 1995 Orioles turned to Ripken, especially as he drew closer to the record. Thom Loverro, in his book, *Home of the Game: The Story of Camden Yards*, said that the original 1995 schedule had Ripken set to break Gehrig's record while the Orioles were on a West Coast swing in Oakland. But the strike had an interesting effect on the Streak, and the shorter 144-game schedule helped the Orioles bring the tying and record-breaking game against the California Angels back to Baltimore.

One rainout would have pushed the record-breaking event out of the city and into Ohio, because the Orioles were scheduled to play in Cleveland the next day. But Maroon said one thing that few people know is that the Indians made a surprising offer to the Orioles during the season.

"The Indians ran away with the [Central] division, and they actually . . . called the Orioles and said, 'If there's a rainout, we'll come to you. He needs to break this at home,'" stated Maroon. "That was really cool and generous. I don't think anyone knows it. They made this offer, and it turned out not to be necessary, but the offer was made. It was a hell of an offer."

Everything continued to build throughout the summer. Maroon said the team was constantly brainstorming ways to make the event special, because they knew this was growing into something very big. One day they came up with an idea that turned out to be a very memorable part of the 1995 season.

A warehouse stood behind the right-field wall and flag court at Oriole Park. The warehouse was huge—it later became the team office location, among other things. Maroon and the Orioles' think tank wanted to use the warehouse wall, in full view of the fans, as a display. The team put up four large numbers that signified where Ripken was in pursuing the streak. Either halfway through or at the end of the fifth inning, they'd cue up some John Tesh music and change the number, signifying that Ripken had added another game to his total.

It didn't go over too well at first. Ripken didn't love it, and some of the fans couldn't figure out what it was. Now, over a decade later, Maroon laughs about it, but he was rather worried at the time.

"We thought this was going to be the coolest thing ever," Maroon said. "But [we said], 'Let's relax. Let's give it some time.' ... I remember Cal telling me how uncomfortable he was with it at first. He thought it was kind of goofy and corny ... "

However, the dropping numbers (which unrolled like a championship banner) became something many, many people looked forward to watching. Fans realized what was coming and loved the music—there were no words, and it was deep, dramatic, and built to a crescendo that became instantly recognizable to Oriole fans everywhere.

Even better was the fact that Ripken himself began to enjoy it. "It ended up getting very emotional for him," Maroon explained. "He'd hear the music, he'd see the number, people would be standing, and then it really got to him and it turned out to be such a great celebration. It built into something that was really emotional for him. The banners were really a cool concept—a neat idea. It came off better than we even imagined it would. It really grew. To this day, you associate the numbers on the warehouse with the Streak."

The numbers—now at the new Sports Legends Museum in Baltimore, right next to Oriole Park—became the thing that people often looked to when coming into the ballpark, and later grew to be the central point of the deeply emotional celebration when Ripken officially broke the record on September 6.

6

BREAKING THE UNBREAKABLE RECORD

Those who followed the Orioles knew this record-breaking game meant little for the team. The Orioles, long out of the hunt, were working on playing out the string. Baltimore came into the game with a 56-65 record, 19 ½ games out of first place, and was already looking to next year. The team had a surprisingly high number of players that wouldn't accomplish much in their careers—a lineup that would change the following year as Baltimore jumped back into contention to win the wild-card spot and make the playoffs for the first time in 13 years.

The Angels needed the game, however. They respected Ripken greatly and what his record meant, but California was holding onto a 5½-game lead that had already begun slipping away. A month earlier, the Angels had an 11-game lead over the Seattle Mariners, who were making a run at their first play-off appearance. The Mariners would pull off the improbable comeback and edge the Angels for the American League West title, but California was trying to hold on when they came to Baltimore in early September.

The Angels won the first of the three-game series before Ripken played in the game that tied Gehrig's mark on September 5. The Orioles seemed energized by the special night, which was emotional in its own right. Baltimore took care of the game quickly, scoring four runs in the second inning—more than enough for starter Scott Erickson, who tossed a three-hit shutout. The Orioles banged out 17 hits in the 8-0 victory.

This was a game filled with home runs for the Orioles, the most dramatic of which came from Ripken, who blasted a solo shot to lead off the sixth. Baltimore hit a total of six homers in the victory, which was punctuated by a special moment midway through the game when Ripken officially tied the Gehrig record.

Ripken's home run was the talk of the town the following day—his timing was amazing and took people's breath away. Yet the record-breaking night would be even more dramatic and unforgettable.

Jim Edmonds, who played for the Angels at the time, said the memories of that evening wouldn't go away any time soon. "What stands out? Just the atmosphere, the celebration of it," he stated. "It was everywhere. It was like being in a mini-World Series. Every day before it, people were selling T-shirts and stuff. The stadium was full. The president was there. It was pretty interesting. It's one of those special things that, when you look back at your career, you'll say that you were there. There are a few things that are like that. I'm happy and lucky to have been a part of it. My dad was there, and he flew in. He understood it, and that's kind of what made me understand it."

Rex Hudler also played on the Angels that night. Hudler usually started against left-handed pitchers, and right-hander Mike Mussina was on the mound for the Orioles. Hudler said he was so surprised to be in the starting lineup that he actually went to then-manager Marcel Lacheman and thanked him for the chance. He still loves looking back on that evening.

"I went into our locker room, and it was really quiet," he stated. "I yelled, 'What's wrong with you guys?' The balls were specially marked, and I wanted a ball, but Larry Barnett, the crew chief, told me they were numbered, and I would have to get a third out to get

Breaking the Unbreakable Record

Ripken blasts a home run against the California Angels. *(Photo by J. David Ake/AFP/Getty Images)*

one. Early in the game, with two outs, a pop-up drifted into shallow right, and I camped underneath it and waved everyone off. Just then, Tim Salmon comes in and calls me off, and I have to peel away. He just laughed, and said, 'This one's mine.' But in the bottom of the fifth with the bases loaded and two outs, Cal comes to bat. He hits this flare that goes over my head. I just started to tear after it, and it was like everything was in slow motion. I reached out and dove and told myself: 'I don't care if I break my face, I'm getting that ball.' When I got up and realized I had caught the ball, I shook my glove because I was so excited. My teammates were all lined up on the rail to give me high-fives, but I ran straight to my locker and put the ball in my briefcase."

Although top starter Mussina pitched for the Orioles, Tim Salmon quickly gave the Angels the lead with a solo homer in the top of the first. Baltimore then tied it in the bottom half when first baseman Rafael Palmeiro answered with his own home run. The game remained tied until Bobby Bonilla started the fourth with a homer off California starter Shawn Boskie. Ripken then homered again, delighting the crowd with a line shot into the left-field seats.

"He did it again! He did it again!" ESPN broadcaster Chris Berman shrieked. But one inning later, Berman did something ESPN announcers don't often do—he kept quiet. Pictures are supposed to be worth a thousand words, and Berman and analyst Buck Martinez both decided to let the network's pictures speak when the game became official and the Baltimore crowd expressed its love for Ripken. Both announcers received huge praise nationwide for their 20-minute silence, and Martinez even won an Emmy Award for Best Sports Special for his work on the broadcast.

The pictures that night spoke volumes.

Everything commenced with the dropping numbers. The Tesh music started, and the cheering began, initiating a near 22-minute celebration. ESPN focused immediately on the numbers on the warehouse wall. When the zero changed to a one and the numbers read "2131," the place erupted. Black and orange balloons—the Orioles' colors—were immediately released into the sky, and the crowd of 46,272 went wild.

Ripken came out of the Orioles' first-base dugout to acknowledge the crowd, which roared in delight. In fact, he walked out several times to answer the fans, but the noise just kept building and building. Ripken then walked over to his wife, Kelly, and their two young children, Rachel and Ryan. He pulled off his white Orioles jersey and revealed a black T-shirt that said "2130 + Hugs and Kisses for Daddy" on the back. He handed them his Orioles jersey and hat, and gave Ryan, just a baby at the time, a high-five that the crowd just ate up.

Standing far above the field were Frank Robinson, one of the greatest players in Oriole history, and Joe DiMaggio. One of the top Yankees on his old team, DiMaggio was also there when Gehrig's streak ended in 1939. He stood with Robinson and watched Ripken's accomplishment with appreciation.

Then there were the signs. They were everywhere. One guy held up the number "21." His friend stood next to him with the number "31." Together, it read "2131" in orange and black. It was simple, but it said it all. One fan draped a sign that said "Ripken Stadium" over the outfield wall. Another held up "The House That Cal Built." Each time Ripken made his way out of the dugout to thank the fans, it seemed that something else caught his attention. It also seemed like he wanted it to stop. The celebration was growing longer and louder, but the Angels had already taken the field to start the bottom of the fifth.

"I guarantee you he wanted the game to continue," Ginsburg said. "There came a point where something else had to happen. There were several minutes of applause because people had been waiting years for this. This was the type of event that words were not going to enhance. You knew what was happening. You knew what was going to happen."

The celebration wouldn't stop. The Orioles stood in their dugout, congratulating Ripken. Everyone came to say something. The Angels appeared in front of their dugout and applauded. Some of the Orioles later said they knew Ripken needed to do something. And then, just like that, the moment turned into one of the most memorable in baseball history.

Ripken sat on the bench next to Palmeiro and Jeffrey Hammonds. Palmeiro playfully draped his right arm around Ripken's shoulders while teammates like Bonilla and others stood nearby, videotaping the moment with their own cameras for posterity. The noise kept building. Finally, Palmeiro and Bonilla pushed Ripken up the steps and out of the dugout along the warning track. Coach Al Bumbry pushed Ripken along a few feet, and suddenly, Cal began trotting down the track along the right field line and thanking a few fans. The roar grew when it became clear he was taking a victory lap. Ripken slowly made his way along the warning track and around the stadium.

Ripken acknowledges the extensive crowd at Oriole Park at Camden Yards.
(Photo by Focus on Sport/Getty Images)

Breaking the Unbreakable Record

"I think, as it turned out, that was about the only thing he was going to be able to do that would get [the crowd calmer]," said his brother, Bill Ripken. "I think Jr. has done the right thing pretty much [all the time] . . . but he had no clue probably that he was going to make a victory lap around the warning track. There was no way that was in his mind. It just looked like it evolved. Once it started, it just couldn't stop until he finished. It was a big moment. I think it ... was awesome. They were so into it."

Cal shook the hands of so many people on the victory lap. He greeted adults, children, Oriole Park workers, policemen, and nearly the entire Baltimore bullpen, who hung over the left-field fence to slap hands with their starting shortstop. One person nearly fell over trying to reach Ripken. Umpires greeted him by California's third-base dugout, and several of the Angels talked with him. Cal hugged some of those he knew, including former teammate Rene Gonzales.

In the end, Ripken made his way completely around the playing field, finally giving the crowd exactly what it wanted. Ripken's father and mother stood watching in a box high above the field. The night had to have been difficult for the elder Ripken after his rough career with the Orioles organization.

But three years later, Cal Ripken Sr. had finally returned to Oriole Park to celebrate his son's achievement. Jr. touched his heart and pointed to his dad, which affected just about everyone who saw it. And his mother stood there with her hands clasped together with pride.

"The lap was the only thing I really liked that night," said Mills. "That was an unbelievable moment that I don't think we'll ever see again, anywhere. He stood out and did the heart thing to his dad. I was watching it from the concourse level from underneath the press box, and I was thinking that we'd never see ... that raw emotion. Maybe we did with Mark McGwire, when he hit 62 and he went over to the Maris family. That was pretty neat. But Cal's was pretty genuine."

Gehrig's record was one that many in baseball had thought to be unbreakable. "Cal Ripken has reached the unreachable star," said Berman on ESPN once the game became official on September 6.

7

LATE-GAME PROBLEMS

B y the later part of the 1990s, there was no question that some of Ripken's skills weren't quite as they had been years before. It was only natural because, well, that's what happens with age. It's also what happens when you try to play every day for about 16 straight seasons.

But it's something that draws more notice on the baseball field when playing shortstop. There's no question that Ripken, at 35, was starting to slow down a bit heading into the 1996 season when Johnson took over as manager. Johnson was somewhat bull-headed and a very intelligent man who wanted to run things his way. In his playing days, he was a very good second baseman for Baltimore and later, Atlanta.

Johnson's Orioles struggled during the first part of 1996. At one point, Johnson said he wanted to move Ripken over to third base and give prospect Manny Alexander a shot at shortstop. Ripken clearly wasn't happy with the move, but Johnson did it anyway, placing Alexander at shortstop on July 15 versus Toronto and shifting Ripken to third. The move didn't work well at all. Ripken didn't like it, and Alexander looked as frightened as a deer in the headlights, getting just one hit in six games before the skipper realized it wasn't working. He moved Cal back, but the move stopped Ripken's streak of consecutive starts playing shortstop at 2,216.

Even though Alexander had ability to field and was quick, he never quite had the hitting prowess to earn a regular spot in the lineup. If he could have been a better hitter, he might have had a shot in the Baltimore lineup. As it was, Alexander never really became a full-time regular anywhere, but has played for parts of 11 seasons (he was still going in 2006 with the Padres). He ended up as a utility player who could fill in at several positions, including second base, shortstop, third base, and right field.

Ripken moved back to shortstop for the rest of that season. Ripken also dodged a bullet after suffering a strange injury at the All-Star Game. The players were together for a pregame picture session when pitcher Roberto Hernandez slipped and his arm swung back, hitting and breaking Ripken's nose. Fortunately, everything stayed in place and Ripken went on to play in the game—along with the others.

But the Orioles were still looking to make a change at shortstop. Ripken had come up to the majors as a third baseman, and the team obviously felt that, at the age of 36, he could play better there. For the 1997 season, the Orioles were interested in Mike Bordick after he had established a solid reputation at shortstop during six years with the Oakland A's.

Bordick was interested, but wanted to make extremely sure that Ripken had no problems with his taking over at shortstop. Bordick has said several times over the years that he didn't want to be playing alongside someone who didn't want him to be there. But there was no problem at all. Ripken understood and easily moved to third. The two played together for about five seasons and gave the Orioles a strong left side of the infield.

"Fortunately, Cal is a great person and helped make that transition smooth for me," Bordick said. "It also helped that year that we had so much success on the field. [Before that], I was probably the luckiest player in the world to play with the Oakland A's [then], People like [then-manager Tony] La Russa, Carney [Lansford], [Dave] Stewart, the list goes on and on of people whom I learned from."

"He and Mike were kind of on the same page with things," Bill Stetka said. "Mike wanted to make sure that Cal was okay with it, and Cal knew what kind of shortstop Mike was. It was almost like he was planning for that stage of his career, to move to third, as opposed to something happening in the middle of the season. You're dealing with two gamers. Cal could see it made them better, so he really had no problem with it in that regard. Bordick is another guy that you have to see every day to realize how good he is. Cal could see that. Cal's the kind of guy who could watch Bordick play nine games for Oakland and see this guy's a really good shortstop. The players have a better understanding of that."

The move first paid big dividends in 1997 when the Orioles took off on a wire-to-wire run that gave them the American League East title and their second consecutive playoff appearance. It also was their first division crown since 1983's World Series championship. Bordick was solid in the field with nine errors and combined with Roberto Alomar to turn 132 double plays. Ripken, meanwhile, had little trouble moving back to third base. He made 22 errors that first season, but those numbers gradually went down over the final few years of his career. He also hit .270 in the regular season and played well in the playoffs. Ripken batted .438 in the four-game division series win over Seattle and then hit .438 in the six-game upset loss to Cleveland in the American League Championship Series.

Ripken later found trouble in a tough 1999 season. The Streak had ended late in 1998, and Ripken's father died just before the new season started. Ripken's back problems pushed him onto the disabled list but when he returned, he truly took off. He hit a career-high .340 despite playing in only 86 games. Ripken did have to undergo back surgery that sidelined him for the final two weeks of the season, but he also ended up with a career best in slugging percentage, .584.

The injuries, however, kept coming in the final years. This was something that Ripken hadn't dealt with as much and it truly slowed him on the field. He addressed the issue at his June 2001 press conference, where he confirmed that the current season would be his last. He pushed himself hard to get back on the field, but realized after all his work that it might be the time to end it.

"The end of last year, I was coming off a period of time when I was out, when I blew my back out again, and if I lump those two years together, they were a struggle physically," Ripken said that day. "[It] resulted in surgery, and last year I pushed it a little too hard in trying to get back, and it blew out again. And as I rested and as I healed, I had to find out where I was physically. I definitely wanted to continue to play, and the last month of the season proved that I should give it a try. So I used the off-season; finally, for the first time in two years, I can make some gains in the off-season. Physically I worked out really hard. As a matter of fact, in hindsight it turned out to be too hard as I broke my rib when I was actually training. But I felt good about the physical side and I really wanted to give it a run to see how I felt physically and where I was and put myself to a test..."

Not being able to play every day in the field was something that seemed to be one of the toughest things for Ripken to deal with in the final part of his career. The Streak had grown into one of the main things people would remember him by, but he simply wanted to play every day—a very simple goal.

When talking to *The Sporting News* in 1995 at the time his son broke Gehrig's record, Cal's father talked about how those things came together.

"It is a tremendous feat. But it's also a burden," he said. "The only thing he wants to do is go out and play a ballgame today, and then turn around and play another one tomorrow. And the next day. So

Late-Game Problems

The longtime ballplayer sits alone in Baltimore's dugout after a rough loss.
(*Photo by Mike Theiler/AFP/Getty Images*)

from that side of it, the Streak takes away from what he really wants to do."

Ripken didn't want to do something that many older players do—see time at designated hitter. He wanted to be out on the field and contribute all the time. Serving as a designated hitter just didn't fit his way of doing things. He wanted to play baseball hard all the time. It was the way he was brought up and the way in which he learned.

As it was, he played only 24 games as a designated hitter throughout his career—all of which came in 2000 and 2001, the final two years of his career.

Most people who followed Ripken's career also knew that he was lucky not have to suffered the serious injuries many others did—especially when playing the difficult position of shortstop so long.

Many also didn't realize how often he endured nagging injuries that wouldn't go away easily because he played every day.

Former manager Frank Robinson also talked about this in his interview with *The Sporting News* in 1995. Robinson grew to understand Ripken's mind-set—he just wanted to play. Nothing more, nothing less.

"Cal is a very special person. He keeps his little injuries to himself," Robinson said in the interview. "He makes the trainer swear he will not tell the manager when he's got a little nick here or a little nick there. He gets his treatment at the times when nobody is around. Even if he has to wait until two o'clock in the morning after a ballgame, he'll get his treatment then and that's it."

The Streak became Ripken's calling card, but in many ways it overshadowed his career, and it made those late-career injuries catch more attention.

But his teammates still wanted him in that lineup every day. Even before Ripken broke Gehrig's record and the calls for Cal to take time off grew louder and louder, teammates—especially pitchers—still wanted him out there. They had confidence in him.

"I guess he didn't start it to go that way. Once the numbers got so high, it was tough to take himself out, obviously," broadcaster Steve Melewski said about the Streak. But he didn't say, 'You had to keep me out there.' It was the managers that kept putting him out there, and like he said of Rick Sutcliffe once, he was going to stop the Streak one day, and he went to Sutcliffe and he talked about it and Sutcliffe said, 'If you sit out tomorrow when I'm pitching I'm going to kill you. You'll be on the front page because you'll be dead because I'll kill you because I need you at shortstop and so does everybody else,' and that's the way his teammates felt about him."

Teammates and opponents never lost that respect for Ripken and his knowledge of the game, even when he slowed down toward the end.

Late-Game Problems

"He knew so much. Because of his dad and his upbringing, he knew the game better than most guys on the team, and he still does," Melewski said. "He can watch a game and see it differently than you or [me] or most guys who know the game well because of his background and so he was always willing to help other guys. He just gives back to the game as a player. He gives back to the game now. And so if we had more like him, it would be a better world and baseball would be a better sport."

Ripken was fortunate that he didn't slide too much toward the end. Some baseball fans can remember the sad sights of Hall of Famer Willie Mays stumbling around the outfield in Oakland while playing for the New York Mets in the 1973 World Series. Although Father Time caught up with him at the end of his game, something that happens to everyone, Ripken remained a force in the Oriole lineup and still could play in the field.

"If you stay injury free for 20 years, eventually it's going to catch up with you," Goldberg said. "He wasn't hitting as well [at the end], he faded at the end. Billy Ripken did the same thing. That's the thing with any aging star. But people didn't expect him to hit .239 [what he hit in his final year], they expected more, they wanted more. After a while you've got to realize your career is over, and then when he realized that, people were for him. I never thought he liked all that attention. That's his personality. He was not a person that liked attention. That's not the way he was."

8

THE STREAK
ENDS QUIETLY

Many wondered how Ripken would actually end the streak when the time came. Would he inform the manager, or vice versa? Most agreed that, barring injury, Ripken would likely get the chance to tell the skipper when one of baseball's most famous streaks would come to an end.

Ripken tied and broke Gehrig's record for consecutive games in a memorable series with the then-California (later Anaheim and now Los Angeles of Anaheim) Angels in September of 1995. He homered on back-to-back days in what turned out to be an unforgettable performance before a national audience. After breaking that record, Ripken simply kept on going.

The Orioles moved Ripken to third base in 1998, and the Streak continued. He passed 2,500 games early in the season for an Orioles team that was having surprising trouble under former pitching coach and new manager Ray Miller. Baltimore had won the American League Eastern Division, going wire-to-wire in 1997 under former manager Davey Johnson. The Orioles beat Seattle during the first round of the playoffs before losing to Cleveland in a mild upset in the American League Championship Series.

Baseball's Iron Man: Cal Ripken Jr., A Tribute

Johnson and Angelos didn't always agree, and the team promoted Miller to take charge in 1998. The team appeared to start well, winning 10 of their first 12 games, but everything soon began to crumble. This was the year that the New York Yankees made mincemeat of everyone, finishing 114–48 and winning their second World Series in three years. But the Orioles never got going after the first few weeks.

Ripken finally did what everyone had been waiting for on September 20, ending the streak that began 16 years earlier. And he did it in a way that most people considered pure Ripken. Miller had put him in the lineup as per usual for this game against the Yankees. But Ripken walked into Miller's office a little while before the game started and told Miller something to the effect of, "It's time." Miller was surprised, but agreed. The Orioles put in highly touted prospect Ryan Minor into Ripken's spot that day, ending Cal's run at 2,632 games.

The Orioles thought Minor could eventually be Ripken's replacement at third base, since Mike Bordick was solidly entrenched at shortstop and would be there for a while. Minor had a low-key personality and, while he understood what the spotlight was, didn't always flourish in it. He went 1-for-4 the evening he replaced Ripken and handled the national media onslaught that came with being a footnote to one of baseball's most famous moments ever, but never really became a big-time performer in the majors.

The move that night shocked everyone, because it wasn't something that many saw coming. Even the lineup card the Orioles used on that occasion showed it was a last-second decision—Minor's name was put into place after Ripken's had been scratched out. Few people noticed the change right away, but when the Yankees saw that Ripken wasn't in the field in the top of the first inning and the same realization began to spread throughout Oriole Park at Camden Yards, the applause began. The Yankees, Orioles, and fans began to cheer, and

The Streak Ends Quietly

Ripken came out to acknowledge it. The Streak was finally over after 2,632 games.

Ripken said later on that he didn't want to end it on the road, and this was the team's final home game of 1998. When his brother got the news from Cal, he wasn't surprised.

"He called me earlier that day. I hadn't been playing," said Bill Ripken. "He called me at home and he said, 'I just want to let you know if you watch the game tonight, I'm not playing.' I said, 'OK.' He said, 'What do you think about that?' I said, 'You always think everything out. I'm not going to tell you not to do it.' Was I surprised? No, not really. It's one of those things that has to come to an end sometimes. And how it comes to an end is a different story. When he called me, it was not a big shocker. This was the day. When he said it, it just kind of rang true. Nice run."

Ripken received an ovation early in the game. He also saw the Yankees on the top step, joining in the ovation—a huge sign of respect for a player who truly asked for nothing else from teammates and opponents.

"People ask me about the secret; I say that it was about an approach," Ripken said. "It was about a sense of responsibility, it was about doing something that you really love to do. Dad certainly gave me that approach, gave me that sense of responsibility, and he guided me."

When Ripken talked with reporters after the game, it was easy to see his emotions, and the way he felt about ending the Streak.

"I just think it reached a point where I firmly believed it was time to change the subject, restore the focus back where it should be, on the team, and move on," Ripken told reporters after the game. "I thought about this for a while, for a long time, and my first inclination was to help the team get to the wild-card berth, to continue to play, keep the focus right on the team, and if we would have fallen through in any way to take the last day off in Boston, just as a way to end it. And then

After playing 2,632 consecutive games, Ripken takes a seat against the New York Yankees. *(Photo by Mitchell Layton/Time Life Pictures/Getty Images)*

The Streak Ends Quietly

I thought about it for a second and through a little conversation with my wife we worked it out and said, 'Wait a minute. If this is going to happen, if this is going to end, let's end in the same place that it started.' It started in Baltimore many, many years ago. Let's do it in my home state, my home city with my family or friends in front of the— and I hope you're listening out there in the stadium—in front of the very best baseball fans anywhere. I appreciate all the support. The only way this is going to be a little bit emotional is it makes me think back on all the great years and all the great times. But this shouldn't be a sad moment. If you look at me, I look at it as a happy moment. It's a celebration. And it's not going to change who I am, it's not going to change the way I approach the game of baseball. I still consider myself an everyday player. And I plan on coming out every single day and proving that on a daily basis. So I'm not going anywhere. All you have to do is look tomorrow and I'll be in the lineup again (Monday) night in Toronto. So that's really it. Don't be sad. Be happy."

Few fans were upset. In fact, they were happy. As the ovation he received certainly showed, they appreciated the fact that they got to see the final moments of the streak at Oriole Park.

"What Cal did is so unbelievable," baseball commissioner Bud Selig said in an Associated Press story that night. "What he's done, he's done a great thing for baseball."

Team owner Peter Angelos also talked about how low-key Ripken remained at the end, even ending the Streak in a way that fit his personality. Some players who demand publicity and love the spotlight would have done it in a different manner, but Ripken handled it all so quietly.

"He just said it very typically Cal," Angelos said in the story. "No melodrama, no emotion. Just flatly, 'This is what I'm going to do.' I know of many injuries he's had, and he's certainly been able to deal with them in a very, very spectacular way. I think he's done the right thing. When you see it happen, you wonder how anyone could have done what Cal has done here. I don't believe anyone will ever equal it. I think Cal has earned his rest."

The rest helped him. Ripken jumped back into the Orioles' lineup the following night when Baltimore went to Toronto to play the Blue Jays. Toronto scored a 3-2 win despite the fact that Ripken, getting back into the game, went 2-for-4.

Ripken's streak had a number of smaller sub-stories. He played 8,243 innings in a row from June 5, 1982 to September 14, 1987, when his father, then the Orioles' manager, pulled him out of a blowout loss. The Orioles were in the midst of an 18-3 defeat at the hands of Toronto. The Blue Jays blasted 10 homers that night, and Ripken agreed with his dad to come out after batting in the top of the eighth inning. Ron Washington replaced him in the bottom half for Toronto's final at-bat.

There also were some other near misses. Ripken hurt his knee when the Orioles and Seattle got into a brawl during a June 1993 contest. But Ripken battled his way through it. Also in 1993, Ripken's wife, Kelly, was pregnant with his son, Ryan. The Oriole had said he'd miss a game if the child were born when the team had to play, but the birth came on an off day.

As it turned out, Ripken made a timely decision to end his streak, because it would have stopped in a different way in 1999. Back problems had often plagued and slowed Ripken, but the biggest difficulty came just before the start of the regular season with the death of Cal Sr. The long-time coach/manager and baseball mentor died of lung cancer. Ripken struggled from the start of the season and finally went onto the disabled list for the first time.

However, when coming back to action later in the spring, Ripken took off. He finished with a career-best .340 batting average and another career high in slugging percentage (.584). But his back problems flared up once more, and he again went onto the disabled list in August, eventually missing the final two weeks of the season when having to undergo back surgery. In the end, Ripken played only 86 games that year.

9

RIPKEN'S FINAL SEASON

A fter his final game as an Oriole, Ripken gave a speech that sums up both his attitude and career. The game meant nothing as the Orioles had long been eliminated from the pennant race. In fact, the Orioles finished with a 63-98 record and barely beat Tampa Bay, who took last place in the American League East. Not much went right for the Orioles that year. Most of the attention was devoted to Ripken's final year as a player once he announced his retirement near the mid-season mark.

Ripken's final game came on Saturday, October 6, 2001, and the Boston Red Sox had little trouble scoring a 5-1 victory over the Orioles. Ripken nearly became the final batter but was left on deck when Brady Anderson, a close friend of Ripken's, struck out to end the game. This upset Anderson, who wanted Cal to have one last at-bat. But the longtime Oriole told his buddy not to worry.

Ripken got a chance to address the crowd of 48,807 shortly after the game. He kept his remarks short, sweet, and simple.

Here's what he said: "As a kid, I had this dream. And I had the parents that helped me shape that dream. Then I became part of an organization, the Baltimore Orioles, to help me grow that dream. Imagine playing for my hometown team for my whole career. And I have a wife and children to help me share and savor the fruits of that dream. And I've had teammates who filled my career with unbelievable moments. And you fans, who have loved the game, and have shared your love with me. Tonight, we close a chapter of this dream—my playing career. But I have other dreams. You know, I might have some white hair on top of this head—maybe on the sides of this head. But I'm not really that old. My dreams for the future include pursuing my passion for baseball. Hopefully, I will be able to share what I have learned. And I would be happy if that sharing would lead to something as simple as a smile on the face of others. One question I've repeatedly been asked these past few weeks is "How do I want to be remembered?" My answer has been simple: to be remembered at all is pretty special. I might also add that if I am remembered, I hope it's because, by living my dream, I was able to make a difference. Thank you."

It wasn't the greatest of seasons for Ripken and could truly be described as an up-and-down year. He finished with a .239 average, by far the lowest of his career, 14 homers, and 68 RBIs in 128 games, ending with a long cold streak that pulled his average down. Ripken battled injury problems. A broken rib sidelined him early in the season, which may have thrown off his timing and forced him to get off to a slow start.

In fact, Ripken struggled from the beginning in 2001. Then-manager Mike Hargrove had talked about reducing the then-40-year-old's role to that of a part-time player, something Ripken clearly wasn't thrilled about—especially considering he had once played in 2,632 consecutive games. But Ripken never got off to a good start before announcing his retirement. Many were ready to throw dirt on Ripken's baseball grave at this point. In addition, Ripken already had committed six errors.

The Orioles set up a press conference in mid-June after word of Ripken's retirement had leaked out the day before. Ripken talked to a large group of media and gave some reasons for his decision, which he admitted was a difficult one that came with a lot of thought and questioning.

"The broken rib kind of set things back a little bit," Ripken said that day. "In hindsight now, I had an abbreviated spring training. I wish [I] would have taken a longer spring training. But I think that is immaterial. I think once we got into the season, some of the things that prompted me to make the decision were the things that were pulling me, you know, toward a decision and toward retirement."

Ripken also said that due to his injuries in the previous seasons, he had been able to spend more time with his children, which he enjoyed a great deal.

"The last couple of years, I've been noticing that I miss being away from home," he said at the press conference. "I miss my kids' activities, and it seemed like the passion, and maybe there was a substitute when I was hurt, but I was getting into other things: My youth initiatives, my teachings, and I found out that my energy and the challenges before me had energized me the same way that baseball did when I walked into the ballpark as a rookie. So I had to kind of place that in an area until I found out for sure what my playing status was. And I think going into the season, I didn't know. I definitely didn't know where things were going to go. I had to play it out to see where it would end up."

There also were a lot of questions concerning his playing. For the first time since he got called up in 1981, Ripken clearly was having troubles at the plate. On the day of the June press conference, Ripken had just a .210 batting average with four homers, and clearly appeared to be losing his punch. But there was no question that making the announcement—maybe even the decision itself—relaxed the future Hall of Famer.

After he told the world that the 2001 season would be his last, Ripken then took off on a streak. He batted .337 (52-for-154) with eight homers and 32 RBIs in his next 42 games. On a curious note, Ripken didn't even hit a homer at Oriole Park until August 14 of that season.

Bill Stetka is the Orioles' director of media relations and publications and has known Ripken for many years. One of the beat writers for the now-defunct *News American*, a longtime Baltimore daily newspaper, Stetka covered the team during Ripken's early seasons, including the Orioles' championship season in 1983. Stetka also served as the team's official scorer for a long time and joined the club to help with media relations in the mid-'90s around the time Ripken broke Gehrig's record. Stetka was in charge of media relations by the time that Ripken decided that 2001 would be his final season.

"In some respects, he didn't want a big ballyhoo, but he also knew there was no way we were going to escape that," Stetka said. "It was much like in 1995, and it was kind of John Maroon's suggestion that we do a first-day interview in every city we went to, get it out of the way the first day, then you don't have to spend all that time at your locker dealing with the media."

And that's the way they did it after Ripken's mid-June announcement. Stetka said this strategy helped Ripken and the Orioles immensely, because it kept a great deal of the media out of the locker room so that the players could simply focus on getting ready for the games.

"The other thing it did was that it took a huge media throng out of the clubhouse and allowed 24 other players to do their job and handle things in a normal way. That, quite honestly, was the [way Cal wanted things]," Stetka said. "Cal was kind of reluctant to buy into the whole thing that all these people want to talk to me and why do we need to do something special. But the aspect of it where we said we move it out to the dugout and we don't have 25 or 30 extra media people clogging the clubhouse [worked out]. He understood and recognized 'if we can make it normal for the other 24 guys, I can put

At the age of 42, Ripken prepares for his final at-bat as a Baltimore Oriole.
(Photo by Stuart Zolotorow)

up with this.' Going back to 1995, recognizing what we did in 1995, we picked up from that and did the same thing. ... I think it helped him, I think it helped everybody, and it gave him a chance to say good bye to everybody."

Stetka said that he talked to Ripken about the best way to handle the fade-out, so to speak. Stetka said the Orioles worked closely with Ripken and Maroon to plan things out and see where they wanted to go. Ripken understood that the media wanted to talk with him but hoped to keep everything as low-key as possible.

The Orioles could feel a hole in their locker room in the 2002 season. Ripken was different than most stars, and didn't want his locker area to be done up in special way. Barry Bonds was well known for his lounge chair and large TV with the San Francisco Giants, but Ripken simply had the corner locker by a door in the back part of the Baltimore locker room.

Stetka said that things felt weird when that next season began. Something seemed to be missing. "You know that there was just this void in his corner," Stetka said. "We kept that area clear for a while. Melvin Mora has since moved into [the] corner, more because of needing the space. The first year was kind of hard to get over and realize that Cal was no longer there. For the first time in over 20 years, there's not a Ripken presence. It took a while getting used to it, and even so, pointing out to new players that would come through. Many hadn't had the experience of being there when Cal was there. I can't tell you how many young guys would say to me at one point or would say to other players, 'Which one was Cal's locker?', which I thought was interesting."

Ripken received a lot of the same attention that Tony Gwynn of the San Diego Padres got that season. Gwynn, considered by most baseball experts to be one of the game's best pure hitters, also announced that he was retiring. Many thought that he and Ripken could be two of the final players who did what many used to do—both played with the same franchise throughout a long and storied career.

"It showed that he was the last of a dying breed, a person who stuck with one team. He could have left but he didn't," said Stan Goldberg, the sports editor for the *Frederick News-Post* in Maryland. "If you stay injury-free for 20 years, eventually it's going to catch up with you. He wasn't hitting as well [at the end], he faded at the end. Brooks Robinson did the same thing. That's the thing with any aging star. But people didn't expect him to hit .239, they expected more, and they wanted more. After a while, you've got to realize that your career is over, and then when he realized that, people were for him. I never thought he liked all that attention. That's his personality. He was not a person that liked attention. That's not the way he was."

10

A BIG HIT

Ripken's final numbers showed that he was a hitter who could do the job both for power and average. Averaged out for a 162-game season of which he played so many, his statistics included 23 homers, 91 RBIs, and a .276 batting average, along with 33 doubles. Ripken was constantly working on ways to improve his hitting skills. Joe Stetka, a longtime baseball coach in Harford County, Maryland, who played high school baseball against Ripken back in the '70s, joked last winter about seeing present Oriole third baseman Melvin Mora at Oriole Park at Camden Yards working on his hitting. He mentioned that Cal would do the same thing.

"Cal Ripken used to hit at least 96 baseballs off a tee all year round," Stetka said. "To me, that's not looking at live pitching, but what he was doing was working on fundamental situational stuff. How to hit the ball to right field, how to take a low inside pitch and turn on it. I think it gives him more credibility. If you're going through a slump...he [could make] adjustments to his stance. It also went to the way he handled himself at the plate. I think it's good for kids to know that Cal Ripken went through a slump."

Much of the criticism that Alex Rodriguez received with the Yankees in 2006 came from his strange refusal to admit he was stuck in a long slump. He said he was doing fine, and spent most of the summer preaching those words to fans and teammates, who became exasperated with them. For some reason, Rodriguez just wouldn't admit that something was going wrong.

But Ripken didn't mind. Like any hitter, he suffered through some long stretches, but worked relentlessly to get his act back on track. Many people who played with or against Ripken will laugh at some point over his tendency to change stances. If you look at certain players, their batting stances are constant. They stay unchanged no matter what game, what time of the year, or what part of their career. While they will work on various techniques before games and in practice situations, they keep their stances the same.

Ripken didn't. If you look at 10 different pictures of Ripken—quite possibly from the same season—you might very well see 10 different stances. If you look at pictures or videos of Ripken from various parts of his career, you might see the same sort of difference. When Ripken struggled later in his career, he adjusted his stance and often found his way.

"I used to tease Billy [Ripken] because Cal would teach the hitting end of their clinics they put on," Stetka said. "I said jokingly that you'll have them all confused, because he played 2,632 games and you'll have them hitting in 2,632 stances, and Billy laughed."

Ripken began his good offensive production early in his career, starting with his first full year in the majors in 1982. The Orioles needed his power, and Ripken bounced back after a slow start to hit .264 with 28 homers and 93 RBIs. His strong hitting played a big role in Baltimore's dramatic late-season comeback, which helped the Orioles pull into a tie with Milwaukee for the American League East lead with one game left in the season—before the Brewers won it on the final day.

Ripken broke out even more in 1983. He played every inning of all 162 games and had one of his best all-around offensive seasons.

Ripken hustles toward home plate. *(Photo by Stuart Zolotorow)*

Ripken fit nicely into the middle of a powerful Orioles' lineup that included Hall of Famer Eddie Murray. The success Ripken found as Rookie of the Year the previous season carried over as Ripken finished with a .318 average, 27 homers, and 102 RBIs. He also led the majors in hits with 211 as the Orioles won the World Series after defeating the Phillies in five games.

Baseballpage.com kept its scouting report on Ripken simple heading into the 1984 season. It said that Ripken "...murders fastballs up and in, hangs tough against curves...will often look at the first pitch to try to see what kind of stuff a pitcher has...is aggressive and confident with two strikes. ...Has very good range, arm strength, and accuracy."

Ripken's numbers had been declining throughout the late '80s, and 1990 brought him to a career-low batting average of .250. After nearly winning the American League East the previous season, the Orioles slipped to a non-contending team once more. But Ripken answered everything in 1991, jump-starting his career once more with a .323 average, 34 homers, plus a career-best 114 RBIs. The talk that he should stop the streak and begin taking some time off to rest his body—now 30 by season's end—grew louder and louder. But he didn't look like a tired player that year. He had 46 doubles and once again became the type of hitter he'd been in his earlier days.

One of the factors that helped Ripken in 1991 was that he once again altered his batting stance. Juan Samuel, who played for several years, knew that Ripken loved to make changes and saw nothing wrong with it.

"That's the sign of good hitters," Samuel said. "A lot of good hitters that I know, [they] have a different approach. He used to work the count where he knew what the pattern of that pitcher is and what he's going to get, and he didn't miss it. That's the number-one thing. A lot of guys get a good pitch, but a lot of times they're going to foul it off or swing right through it. He didn't miss most of them when he was sitting on something and he got it. All of that comes with being a student of the ballgame. He did his homework on who he's facing. I had a few guys tell me that he used to really see who the umpire was behind the plate and know what their tendencies were. You don't see a whole lot of guys trying to do that."

Samuel said the fact that Ripken looked so hard to get so many advantages actually gave him an edge—one he rarely failed to use.

"He had the upper hand," Samuel said. "You'd probably want to pitch around him and do other things, hopefully you'd face whoever was behind him and have that guy beat you. You always have a couple of guys in the lineup that you're going to say, 'I'm not going to let this guy beat me in a key situation,' and Rip was one of those guys."

Jose Rijo was a powerful pitcher during his days in the majors and is known by many for his strong work in 1990, when the Cincinnati Reds shocked the baseball world by beating the heavily favored Oakland A's in the World Series. Rijo won two games in that Fall Classic, including Game 4 of the four-game sweep, when he threw $8\frac{1}{3}$ innings in Cincinnati's 2-1 victory.

The 6-foot-2, 200-pound Rijo never backed down from any batter, and he kept up that aggressiveness in his new role with the Washington Nationals' front office. When talking about Ripken, Rijo shook his head. It was easy to hear the admiration in his voice.

"I [loved] the way he played the game, his aggressiveness," Rijo said. "The reputation he built around himself, it was just outstanding. Even before you faced him, if you never faced him before, you heard that he [could] do so much, everybody told you to be careful of this guy, and you'd be afraid. If you're a rookie, to see him at the plate, imagine seeing him swinging the bat. He was a dead fastball hitter. I was a good slider pitcher. That guy was so fucking great."

While in the clubhouse at a Washington game midway through the 2006 season, Rijo talked about Ripken as if he were still a pitcher trying to figure out how to get out a very tough batter.

But Ripken was a batter he clearly didn't love to face.

"You know, he worked the count to his advantage looking for the fastball," Rijo said. "One thing about him, if he got the pitch he wanted, he made sure he didn't miss it. I'll tell you what, no matter what I say about Cal Ripken, I can never say enough. The guy was a great level hitter, a hard worker, passionate for the game, a lover of the game. There's not enough I can say to make a [good] description of his image. I'm still going to be short in one way or the other, when [it comes to] anything I can say about Cal Ripken. The guy was perfect on and off the field, and it showed. It's easy for me to say now. But I know that somewhere in there I'm missing something."

Ripken's 1991 season was as close to perfection as he ever found during his career. People had already begun saying that the Streak was a part of the reason some of his offensive numbers were going down. But that strong year silenced some of the critics—for a while.

One of the biggest moments for Ripken that year came during the All-Star Game in Toronto. He blasted 12 homers in the Home Run Derby. He then won the MVP award the next day in the All-Star Game, as his three-run homer played a big role in the American League's victory.

Ripken had some more big seasons at the plate, but that year was his best. But with all the attention that came from the Streak, so many people missed the fact that Ripken grew into a consistent home run hitter. In many ways, he was just like his good friend Eddie Murray. Neither player ever had a wildly incredible year at the plate throughout their long careers—yet both were so good when their teams desperately needed them. They had power and the ability to hit in the clutch. But both had such low-key personalities on the field and in person that they flew under the radar.

Longtime Baltimore broadcaster Steve Melewski said Ripken's offensive numbers would have pushed him into the Hall of Fame even if the Streak had never taken place.

A Big Hit

"If there was never a streak, Cal would still be a Hall of Famer—400 home runs, 3,000 hits, count the number of players who have done that, I think it's eight now," Melewski said. "If you're one of eight in the history of the game to have put up those numbers and you were a Gold Glove shortstop and you revolutionized the position by being a tall shortstop, one of the first ever, that's first-ballot Hall of Fame material with or without a streak. Cal is known for the Streak, and he knows it will live with him forever. He can't ever lose that legacy, and he's proud of it. But I think people should realize he was a Rookie of the Year, he was an MVP, he won the World Series, he hit 400 home runs and he had 3,000 hits, and when they count the roll of the players who have done that, it's a small class."

Melewski said that Ripken remained a consistent player, and that's why people in the game respected him so much. But he also said that Ripken's average could have been higher if he opted to sit out a few games a year against tough pitchers. However, that never happened.

"He never was the dominant offensive player of his time or even of a year," Melewski said. "Maybe occasionally he was right there. But he never had a dominant year like Bonds or a McGwire or anybody like that. But he was just steady and consistent and to put up the numbers he put up, it's more than longevity. He'll probably go into the Hall of Fame with one of the lowest career batting averages, but again, remember the position he played and remember that he played every day and he didn't sit out against tough right-handers. That's where that might have improved his batting average 10 or 20 points in a year if he sat out against the tough righties. He took on all comers because he played every day and he never missed a pitcher, whether it was an ace starter or a closer or anybody. He could have sat out 10 games a year against tough righties, and his average would have been higher."

11

CHANGING THE IMAGE OF SHORTSTOP

O ne of the biggest effects that Ripken had in his baseball career was the way he changed how the sport looked at shortstops. Before the 6-foot-4 Ripken took over as Baltimore's regular shortstop during the 1982 season, most who played the position were short, quick, skinny, and could cover the wide range that shortstops must handle on a regular basis. Shortstops must be quick to both get to the hole and make their way to balls up the middle. Oriole history includes smaller players like Luis Aparicio, who anchored the infield at shortstop en route to the 1966 world championship. Mark Belanger took over after Aparicio, and became one of the most recognized shortstops in the major leagues. Belanger struggled at the plate for long stretches in his career, but was well known for his ability to cover his position. He combined with Brooks Robinson to give the Orioles one of the greatest left sides of the infield in baseball history.

But Ripken initially came to the Orioles as a third baseman, which is where he began his first full year with Baltimore in 1982. However, longtime manager Earl Weaver was one who never worried about doing things differently. Weaver was one of the first managers to keep statistics on how batters and pitchers fared against each other—something that's the norm rather than the exception today.

Weaver had watched Ripken for a number of years as he grew up. Ripken went to Memorial Stadium and endlessly took ground balls from his father, a man who believed passionately that fundamentals help players build their skills up to higher levels. The skipper watched Ripken develop and saw something that made him think "shortstop."

"The organization had thought he'd be a third baseman. When you have a guy who's going to hit you 20 to 25 home runs and drive in 80 runs and he can field the position, he's definitely shortstop material. It was just as simple as that," Weaver told *The Sporting News* in a 1995 interview when Ripken was about to break Gehrig's record.

Weaver wanted to move Ripken to shortstop right away in 1982, but battled some people in the organization who, along with many others, didn't think that a long, tall kid who didn't have much speed could actually play shortstop. But Weaver kept pounding and pounding and finally moved Ripken to the position on July 1.

The move surprised many at first. Ripken struggled a little initially, but eventually settled in without too much trouble. He used his brain to help make up for any physical deficiencies, such as his lack of quickness. No matter what happened, Ripken seemed to find a way to get to where the ball would be hit. He also kept in place the long-standing baseball philosophy that all good teams must be defensively strong up the middle.

But interestingly enough, Ripken didn't seem to get the attention Weaver and many others felt he deserved for his defensive work. Although most baseball followers always gave Ripken credit for being solid in the field, he didn't seem to gain national notice until midway through his career.

This came in 1991, during Ripken's second Most Valuable Player season. The Orioles struggled all year, but Ripken finally broke through in terms of defensive attention. He won his first Gold Glove after registering 528 assists, the second-highest in his career, making just 11 errors, and posting a .986 fielding percentage. Ripken then came back to win his second straight Gold Glove award in 1992. Although he never won the award again for his play at shortstop or third base, these victories were probably made sweeter by the fact that Ripken didn't win the award in 1990 despite spectacular numbers and just three errors.

Ripken's career fielding numbers were also strong. He played 2,977 games in the field and finished with an impressive .977 fielding percentage. Players appreciated how strong Ripken could be in the field and the way he helped the Orioles, who often struggled or had a number of inexperienced players.

"The fact of the matter was that he was always there," said Tom Paciorek, who played against Ripken and the Orioles in the '80s. "And if you hit a ball in the hole, and you thought that you had a base hit between shortstop and third, Cal would be standing there, and you don't know why he got there or how he got there. Next time up, you might hit a ground ball up the middle pretty hard, and you think you've got a base hit, and then he's standing there again."

Paciorek and others are amazed at how Ripken used his knowledge to do his job better. Understanding various things, like putting himself one step closer to the hole or to the middle based upon what the pitcher would throw or how the batter was known to hit, made him that much more adept.

When talking about Ripken, Paciorek laughed in admiration and partial disbelief. "I thought his knowledge and his ability to read the batter, and put that in conjunction with what the pitcher was doing on the mound, made him an absolutely great shortstop," Paciorek said. "The biggest shortstop you could ever imagine."

John Valentin had many battles against Ripken during his long career with the Boston Red Sox. Valentin agreed with Paciorek as to what made Ripken such a great shortstop.

"He was definitely a smart player. He played a long time," Valentin said. "He was a captain on the infield. He was a guy who

At 6-foot-4, Ripken changed the way Major League Baseball viewed the position of shortstop. *(Photo by Focus on Sport/Getty Images)*

could read the opposition's players, their strengths and their weaknesses, and know what the strengths and weaknesses of his pitching staff ... and what they could do, whether they could hit their spots, whether they could miss their spots, and ... he could be in the right place in the right time."

In fact, Ripken's huge success at shortstop changed the way that many in the sport looked at the position. It opened the door for players like Derek Jeter and Alex Rodriguez—bigger guys who could serve as power hitters yet still play a position that had once been reserved for smaller players. Both players have repeatedly talked about how much Ripken's success paved the way for them.

Juan Samuel is a past infielder who saw and appreciated how well Ripken played on a regular basis. "Well, I know for me, being often in the National League, you hear the names of players who are good and some of them whom you don't get to see or you see a little bit in spring training ..." Samuel said. "But for me, when I came over to the American League and I saw Rip, I was like, 'Well, can this big guy play shortstop, really?' Your typical middle infielder was a little guy, quick hands, kind of quick feet, and to see him basically change how people looked at that position and play it as well as he did because for us, it's like, 'Does he have the range because he's so big? Maybe he'll be a third baseman.' One thing that I noticed from him is that he really knew the pitchers, and he knew how to move with pitches and little things like that, probably to make up for, well, I'm not saying a lack of range or quickness for that particular position, which is something that you ... see with guys like Alex Rodriguez and big guys now, and the little guys are not necessarily the shortstops, and I think he had a lot to do with that."

Samuel said it would be nice to see more players do what Ripken did, using their cerebral skills combined with their physical skills to become better athletes. In the faster paced world in which we live, not as many players think about nor want to do this.

But Samuel, now a minor-league manager, agreed that he'd love to see more players understand the importance of this and how it can help their games.

"You wish you could see more guys do that. You could have the ability, but sometimes that ability can only take you so far and then the mental part of the [game] has to take over, and I think that with Cal, that's what separated him from most of the shortstops, because he was a very smart baseball player playing defense and on offense as well," Samuel said. "I think he was playing the game beyond his time. Obviously, shortstops in his day didn't hit for power or extra-base hits, and it was more of a glove-type position. ... He was one of the very few in the beginning who could hit for power and for average and be in the middle of the lineup. That's where Alex Rodriguez, who was a big guy, and a young player, who came in with the same kind of height and weight and basically played that position from an offensive point of view as well. He definitely proved he could play the position as well."

Most shortstops, in addition to being known and looked at for their defensive skills, weren't counted on much for offense, or if they were, they mainly had a good average and scored some runs. Rare was the shortstop who hit for power on a consistent basis. In baseball, it just wasn't something that happened very much. Players like Ozzie Smith, who first drew attention during the early days of his career with a poor San Diego team before catching national notice after being traded to St. Louis, was known for his spectacular defensive skills. He didn't get nearly as much notice for what he did at the plate, except for a big home run he hit against Los Angeles in the 1985 playoffs.

But Ripken shook things up. In addition to being the biggest shortstop most had ever seen, he also became the best power hitter in a position that people noticed. He wasn't like most shortstops who hit a handful of homers—if that many—each season. Instead, Ripken made people in the sport scratch their heads and change their thoughts concerning a shortstop's capabilities.

"He was the biggest shortstop that you could ever imagine," Paciorek said. "He was the guy you always wanted up there in the ninth inning. He and Eddie Murray were the guys they wanted up there to have a chance to win. He was the guy; he'd drive in the big run. But he didn't have the prettiest swing. He wasn't the most gifted athlete of that era."

Ripken also used that intelligence that helped him on defense to assist him at the plate. "He was a very smart baseball player on offense as well," Samuel said. "I used to see him with a different stance every time we came to town. I'm like, OK, we're going to Baltimore, and I'm going to see which one Ripken is going to throw up there today. But to make those adjustments so quickly ... as you know, it takes guys time to get used to different stances. But it seemed like he did it every time we came to town."

Samuel, who laughed at the way Ripken, a perfectionist, continued his never-ending pursuit for the perfect stance, understood the Baltimore shortstop's search.

Samuel said that, while some players often stick with the same stances, others keep changing to find something that's comfortable and good. And when they discover that batting stance, it's not only a plus for them individually, but also for their team.

"That's the sign of good hitters," Samuel said. "A lot of good hitters that I knew, [they had] a different approach. He used to work the count where he knew what the patterns of that pitcher [were] and what [he was] going to get and he didn't miss it. That's the number-one thing. A lot of guys get a good pitch, but a lot of times they're going to foul it off or swing right through it. He didn't miss most of them when he was sitting on something and he got it. All of that comes with being a student of the ballgame. He did his homework on who [he was] facing. I had a few guys tell me that he used to really see who the umpire was behind the plate and [knew] what their tendencies were. You don't see a whole lot of guys trying to do that."

That's the way Ripken wanted to play the game. He was an observant person who did his research in order to be the best player possible so the Orioles could win. That was his bottom line—do the best you can to help find success.

But this also led to a lack of flair that kept him under the radar in a number of ways. He played the game without flash and dash, something so many players in this day seem to live for and desperately crave. That wasn't how Ripken did things, especially in the field. Former Oriole teammate and roommate, Floyd Rayford, summarized this fact very succinctly when talking about what Ripken did to the game and for the shortstop position.

"I always thought he changed the way people looked at shortstops, because now you've got a [6-foot-4] guy out there, 235 pounds out there, and that's not your typical shortstop, that's a third baseman," said Rayford, now a minor-league coach in the Minnesota organization. "Cal had great hands, [he really had] soft hands for an infielder. Cal did a lot of things to save himself on the longevity side. He rarely threw the ball over the top. I think the way he started throwing [helped]. He went from a position [that involved] basically looking in the stands to being involved in every play. That's what's so impressive."

Rayford said that, despite all the attention that came with Ripken's move to shortstop, the players on the 1982 team weren't bothered much by it.

"I don't [think] they worried about it so much," Rayford said. "If you're missing a lot of balls at third base, a person's going to say, 'How the hell's he going to play shortstop?' It's not like he was missing a lot of balls at third base. I think Cal always positioned very well where he didn't have to go great distances in a big hurry. I think his dad always had him where he needed to be. It's a little guy position, but [Ripken showed] you could put big guys there."

12

SETTING THE TONE

There was no question that anyone who worked with or knew Cal Ripken understood what he valued on the baseball field—hard work. Ripken said numerous times that he viewed what he did as a job, and he wanted to show up at his place of employment every day and give his best effort. It didn't matter where the Orioles were in the standings; Ripken never wavered.

Maybe that's why the Streak caught the attention of so many. The celebration involved paying tribute to a man who just wanted to do his job. Nothing more, nothing less. So many fans who followed the game understood and empathized with him. So many fellow teammates and players did also.

Those who played with Ripken on the Orioles over the years said he was a leader. But he wasn't the kind of guy who came into the locker room yelling and screaming or getting in a person's face about this or that. Rather, Ripken let his work speak for itself. He had a plan every day that he rarely deviated from, and he used it to give his best performances.

Rayford roomed with Ripken on road trips during the early days of Cal's career. Rayford, a utility infielder who played with the Orioles off and on from 1980-87, is now a coach in the Minnesota Twins' minor-league organization. He said that Ripken kept a certain pattern all the time.

"Cal just used to stay in this routine," Rayford said. "He'd eat at the ballpark after the game. He'd go back to the room. I always went out a lot, but he'd go back to the room. He'd probably sleep until two o'clock the next afternoon, then get up and go have lunch and go to the ballpark. He slept a lot. He just never went out a lot. To me, I just thought he was always focused on baseball. We tried, but we just couldn't get him to go out."

Rayford emphasized that there was nothing wrong with it. Ripken simply went about things in a certain way.

"The thing that I know about him is he's a very programmed kind of guy," Rayford said. "He has a certain routine that he does and sticks with."

But Rayford—and others—said that Cal loved to goof off. He enjoyed wrestling and rolling around in the hotel, in the locker room, and everywhere else. The Ripken brothers often joked around and were very physical, but Rayford said he was also one of the players who caught the brunt of it.

"When he did wake up, all he wanted to do was wrestle," Rayford said with a laugh. "He'd come over and see if you were awake, and see if you wanted to wrestle. I would kick his ass every day, but when he leans on you it's tough, once he starts [wrestling] it's tough."

Rayford still laughs about the wrestling.

"It was every road trip, every day," he said. "He'd go to the park, he'd come … looking for me. We'd punch each other for five, 10, 15 minutes and [pitching coach] Ray Miller would be over in the corner saying, 'Oh, God, they're going at it again.' I'd hit him in the ribs, and he'd hit me in the ribs, and his punches were just so heavy. After a while … it tends to wear you down. We'd do this sometimes 10 minutes before the games would start."

Rayford said with a laugh that people just rolled their eyes when he and Ripken would go at it—and they'd go at it often over the years. In fact, it was a habit that just kept going. The two former roommates ran into each other in December 2005 in Baltimore at the funeral of longtime Oriole coach Elrod Hendricks. When seeing each other at the church, they started to jokingly punch each other.

"I try to stay at least 10 feet from him," Rayford said with a laugh. "But I'll tell you, when he sleeps, he's out, he's gone. When he gets up, the guy has so much energy, it's just all day."

That energy was one of the things that helped him become a leader. Ripken just didn't want to stop. It wasn't an obsession. It was just the way he went about things, the quintessential definition of the term "workmanlike."

His teammates have all kinds of stories. Catcher Chris Hoiles, who was inducted into the team's Hall of Fame in 2006, talked about the time that Ripken became irritated with the way the coaching staff or manager was calling pitches in a road game one day. So the infielders and Hoiles all gathered together on the mound with a rather angry Ripken, who informed them that he'd be calling pitches for a little while. And so he did. He just took charge.

Hoiles said that Ripken was the type of person who led by example. It wasn't about how to get the big hit or how to make the right play—it was the way in which Ripken went about his craft. He worked harder than anyone on the team when he never had to worry about losing his position. Ripken just kept wanting to get better and better. It was an insatiable appetite he had, something that drove him to success.

But it also drove others on the team. They saw what he did and how much practice and work he put in. Everyone noticed—how could you not? And it was something that drove other players, including Hoiles, whose hard work made him a much better player than anyone expected when Baltimore acquired him from Detroit. Hoiles often had to fight for his job at the start of the season, yet never lost it, and if an injury hadn't cut short his career a few years too soon, his final statistics would have been that much more impressive.

"He just wasn't a vocal guy, and you don't have to be," Hoiles said. "And [there are] a lot of people who say you have to be and that's how you lead a team, and that's not true. Cal led this team by who he was and what he did and his work ethic, not only during the season but off-season; the guys that took his lead really benefited from that. Trying to keep up with Cal was a chore. He was a continuous worker, the things that he did, the level that he did it and all this other stuff. If you followed Cal, it raised your game. It helped me, and it helped more people than I could mention, but I followed him. I watched him. I tried to emulate him. I tried to do the things that he did, the way that he did it. It ultimately helped me because I'm in the batting cages more, I'm taking more ground balls at first, it's just kind of a tireless attitude through Cal."

Opponents noticed it also. Bert Blyleven had one of the greatest curveballs any major-league pitcher ever threw. His was a backbreaking bender who caused batters many problems. But when playing against Ripken several times during his 22-year career, Blyleven got a good look at how the Oriole legend went about things.

"I always admired Cal Ripken for what he stood for on the baseball field," Blyleven said. "He was someone that played hard day in and day out, never missed a game. The way that he went about his business was great. He was highly respected as a player and a person. He was a true role model, I think, to the Oriole organization and to everybody that ever wore a major-league uniform."

Blyleven also said that it carried over to the way Ripken played during the Streak. He liked the fact that Ripken didn't take shortcuts and kept playing the game hard every day in every city.

"All his hits and the way he played the game were great," Blyleven said. "He wasn't one that took the Streak to say, 'OK I'm going to play

Setting the tone for the rest of the team, Ripken displayed constant intensity as an Oriole. (Photo by Ronald C. Modra/Sports Imagery/Getty Images)

five or six innings,' he played all nine. I saw Cal Ripken play. He went out for the first inning, and he'd be there for the ninth."

Bruce Cunningham has been with the Baltimore Fox TV station since it began reporting news in 1990. As the sports director, he dealt with Ripken numerous times over the years and learned a great deal about what the player thought and how he went about his activities.

Cunningham said one thing was very simple—the ballpark was Cal's office and people were expected to act in an appropriate manner there. There just was no other option.

"He was at that ballpark to work, and you were not to interfere in any way," Cunningham said. "He was so regimented. Everything he did he had a schedule for, and he was not about to deviate from that schedule. Nothing was left to chance with Cal. It was like a businesslike approach rather than a competitive approach, that's what I felt. There wasn't a lot of nonsense that you could see. Behind the scenes, he'd joke around. You saw very little twinkle in his eyes."

Cunningham stressed that Ripken wasn't a bad or mean person in any way. He just had a way he wanted to go about doing things. This was his job and nothing would deter him from giving his best effort.

"He wanted to play all nine every night. It was all about the routine," Cunningham said. "It was not just set in concrete. It was concrete set in granite. I've got things I need to do, and I'm going [to do them]."

Cunningham and others marveled at how Ripken stuck to his way of doing things. This author once was scheduled to interview Ripken for a story for the Orioles' game program, but team officials weren't exactly sure when to hit Cal during his schedule—so I got a three-day pass—even though the article was for the team.

But Ripken liked to do things his way. Maybe it gave him comfort. Some players are that way. However, Ripken never budged from his routine and people understood that, although it occasionally made things difficult with the media. But local people understood that it was nothing personal if Ripken got flustered.

"He remained that way throughout his career, and he got better with the media as time went on," Cunningham said. "Cal likes to think about what he says. If somebody asked him a tough question or a question that was all hearts and flowers, he'd chuckle. He was never rude to us, but he wasn't somebody you were just going to get a quote from. He had a regal presence. He was aloof, but not aloof in a bad way. If you look up the actual definition of aloof, that's what he was, but nobody had a problem with that."

In addition, Cunningham said that Rick Sutcliffe told him an interesting tale that showed how difficult things were at times for Ripken. Sutcliffe said that no matter how big he got, he could always go home and just be Ricky. Ripken couldn't even do that because this wasn't just the town where he played baseball, but also his hometown. It was a double-edged sword that proved painful at times because there weren't many—if any—places that Ripken could go in order to escape.

But Cunningham and most others agreed that Ripken has loosened up a bit, especially with the media, since his retirement. Cunningham agreed that Ripken loves to talk about the programs he does for children and his father.

Dealing with the media on a nightly basis could be difficult, but not having to answer all the questions now makes things better.

"He's not playing anymore and he doesn't feel the pressure anymore," Cunningham said. "It was the same story that he was having to deal with night after night after night. He just had to go through with it."

Cunningham and others said Ripken wasn't the type of player that some reporters felt easy to approach on a regular basis. Every team has a few individuals who will always talk to the media and give a quote on something or other. Brian Roberts is one of those guys on the present-day Orioles. But Ripken viewed being at the ballpark as having a job to do and wanted to concentrate on that whenever possible.

"I never had problems with him," Cunningham said. "He had a very regal presence. Over the years, he made his peace with it. Now that he's not playing, he's a little looser, he's not as tense as he was. I think he's at a stage in life now, he's got his two dreams, he has his own club, and he can teach kids. But here's the thing. I never stopped getting a tingle when I walked past him. That continues to this day."

Ripken's aware of who he is and what he became in the game of baseball. Talk to anyone who played or coached against Ripken, and they'll speak in almost hushed, admiring tones of his unyielding desire to keep working and keep getting better.

Davey Lopes knows exactly what it takes to be a very good middle infielder, because he was one himself for a long time in the major leagues—16 years, in fact. Lopes later went on to become a coach and manager for different teams. After working with the Washington Nationals, he will start the 2007 season as a coach with the Phillies.

Lopes played during Ripken's time and coached with the Orioles while Cal was on the team. He has a good understanding of what pushed the man to, well, keep pushing.

"His work ethic is unsurpassed. I guess he gets that from his father because they were old school, basically," Lopes said. "His thing was, 'I'm going to work, I'm getting paid, so I'm going to play.' I don't ever remember him, in the three years I was there, even anticipating a day off or wanting a day off."

Lopes said that Ripken was a very strong individual, probably more mentally than physically. Lopes also called the Streak a tremendous accomplishment. Ripken received plenty of criticism as the Streak grew, especially from people who said he cared more about it than helping the Orioles.

But Lopes, like many others who were associated with the Orioles during the later part of the Streak, waved off that talk.

"It's always so easy to criticize people from afar," Lopes said. "People don't know, they say what they would do in that situation, but you put most people in that same situation, they're going to play. When you're in reach of a record, I don't know any individual that's going to say I don't want it, I'm going to sit down, I'm not going to play, I'm not going to get a hit tonight because I've got 55 consecutive [hits], and I don't want to break Joe DiMaggio's mark or hit 754 home runs, and I don't want to tie Hank Aaron. The athlete wants to play and perform and compete. He epitomized what an athlete is. He is a role model, but I don't think he looks at it that way. If you're going to look up to someone or have your game not so much compete with his but emulate, you couldn't pick a better guy. I don't know what they do in Baltimore now, but when I was in Baltimore, we took infield every day, and he didn't ask for any special privileges, maybe, out of the three years, he may have missed infield twice, maybe three times. When you have your star athlete out there doing what everybody else does, it makes it a lot easier on the manager as far as disciplining other players. I mean, if Cal Ripken is doing it, how can anybody else say, 'I don't want to do it'? Here's a guy that was going after one of the elite records in baseball. I was in awe of him from that standpoint, his work ethic was unsurpassed by anybody that I have ever seen play the game."

Bill Stetka is in charge of the Orioles' media relations now, but has also seen Ripken from other angles. He was a reporter with the now defunct *Baltimore News-American* when Ripken came up in the early '80s. He agreed with Lopes that Ripken's mind was on the game when he came to the ballpark. He loved having fun in the clubhouse, but always had a plan in place to play that day.

"There was the business side of Cal which I don't think he ever let affect whatever happened between the lines," Stetka said. "The other thing with him was that in spite of the Streak and everything that went on, [you saw] him every day in the clubhouse just rough-housing and clowning around with the clubhouse kids, the batboys, with Brady, with other guys. They got into full-scale wrestling matches and [chased] each other down and playing town and [rolled] over couches. A guy that was so consumed by the Streak wouldn't be doing something like that. That's why I don't think he ever let the fun aspect of it dictate playing or not playing. It was still a game. He still wanted to have his fun. There were times when, if you look at Billy Ripken, Billy certainly had a lot of injuries throughout his career. Billy had more fun. Billy is more of the joker. I think where the Streak may have affected Cal was probably in [not] allowing some of his real personality to show. I think he became such a spokesperson for baseball and everything else that was going on. I think there were times where he became a little bit too guarded about what he would say and how he should say something ... where Billy was free to kind of go off on a tangent and say some things. I think Cal kind of looked at it, and kind of measured his words some. Cal has gotten kind of different since he's been out. He's much more effusive now.

Former major-leaguer Tom Paciorek said that he admired Ripken for playing every day for the simple reason that there had to be times when he just didn't feel right. It happens to everyone, but Ripken found a way to keep going—for 2,632 games. Almost everyone who has played the game just shakes their head in awe at this, simply because he was able to keep going out and doing his thing for so long.

"He wasn't the most gifted athlete of that era. How do you show up and play every day like that?" Paciorek said. "He had to be sick like that. He had to be sore. He had to be aching. But he showed up and did his job, and that was back in the day when they took infield all the time. I don't think I ever was in Baltimore where he didn't take infield, and I'm thinking, 'What? It's 150 degrees out here. How do you do that? Isn't that amazing?' I think he took such pride in the game. I knew his dad a little bit. I just got the biggest kick out of him. Cal Sr.

was real fun to talk to. If you [could] catch him aside, he was an encyclopedia of knowledge that you could gain from him, and I'm sure that's where Cal got his training and, of course, his discipline to be able to do that. I think the mental part of Cal's game was certainly much stronger than his actual physical game."

Paciorek meant that last statement as a compliment. If you talk to anyone who saw or played with Ripken, they'll all say similar things. If Ripken was a Terrell Owens-type of personality, it would be one thing, but he never wanted the spotlight and never sought the grand stage. He just wanted to go out and play ball every day the way he was taught.

13

CHARACTER

In the present-day, no-holds-barred world of electronic and Internet journalism, never-ending talk shows and post-it sites, very little can be hidden if you're a star. There's always something unflattering about someone—except for players like Cal Ripken Jr.

Ripken was so well known and loved in the Baltimore area and later nationally that he is rarely criticized. About the only bad things people will say are that maybe he pushed the Streak too hard, should have sat out some more games, and yes, his range was more limited in the final years of his career.

Maybe this is because of Ripken's personality. Growing up in Harford County, he is the ultimate small-town guy who's unfailingly polite to this day. When doing an interview with me, for example, he strenuously apologized at the start because he showed up late—eight minutes late, to be exact.

As Ripken's stature in baseball grew to a level that no one could have imagined, his personality didn't change. If asked to do something with baseball for kids, he'd often do it. Dealing with the media was an experience, but more often than not, he'd get through it.

Steve Melewski was a longtime broadcaster with WBAL Radio, the Orioles' longtime flagship radio station. He's now moved on to become the voice of Ripken's IronBirds, and has gotten to know the man well. Melewski thinks that the former Oriole behaves in a manner that many could learn from.

"One of my favorite Cal stories was when, one day, my boss wanted me to do a story on interleague play and a lot of the players didn't want to talk about it because it was boring to them," Melewski said. "I went up to Cal and said, 'Can I ask you two or three questions on interleague play?' Cal said, 'You know, I can't do it right now, catch me later in the homestand.' I walked away thinking, well, that meant Cal didn't want to do it, and I wasn't going to get Cal. The next day, I get a tap on the shoulder. It's Cal. He said, 'Hey, do you still want to do that interview? I've got a few minutes.' He remembered, he took me to his locker, he gave me five minutes, great answers, exactly what I needed … whereas a lot of players were like, 'Nah, I don't want to be bothered.' He remembered and came to me. That's the kind of guy he was. And if he ever had to turn you down it was very polite."

Joe Stetka said Ripken has remained the same over the years and has taken his down-to-earth personality with him, especially when working with children. It's important to connect with kids, and Ripken knows how to do it.

"He's wonderful with kids," Stetka said. "Just his presence, knowing what he stands for, that he was a clean ballplayer, he was an everyday ball player, hurt or limping. He was always there. He was in the lineup every day because that's what his father taught him. You're in the lineup, you play. I guess it's … an old cliché. There's always somebody behind you, over your shoulder, looking for that opportunity. That's what I really liked about the guy. He's a big kid, still. No one can ever take that away from him. I'm still a big kid. We all are. But he's a guy that I look up to because of what he stands for, all of it's good."

Mike Hargrove had the unenviable task of cutting Ripken's playing time down in the final two seasons of his career. He had to tell Cal that

the Orioles were going to look at more of the younger players—
something that didn't always sit well with a man who made history for
playing in 2,632 consecutive games.

Hargrove spoke to the media the night of Ripken's final game and
gave a surprisingly candid comment as to what the skipper would take
with him from managing the future Hall of Famer in 2001.

"[It was] probably the time I saw his famous stubborn side, or his
ability to rise up and meet a challenge," Hargrove said that night. "We
were in Tampa Bay and word had leaked out that I was going to restrict
his playing time. At the time, Cal was struggling and we had some
young players we needed to see. Cal wasn't real happy about it and I
didn't expect him to be, but we had a very positive discussion, not
animated at all, and we talked about what his role would be and what
we were trying to do. It was a very positive encounter, and I'll always
remember that."

Hargrove also said he had been fortunate to be around a number
of Hall of Fame players in his career, but never had dealt with someone
who received such respect everywhere. He said that Ripken earned
admiration locally, nationally, and around the world—the level of
which just amazed Hargrove.

This respect also showed up in other ways. Frank Wren had been
the Orioles general manager for just one season before he was fired
after the 1999 season. Wren clashed with upper management on a
variety of issues, including an incident that involved Ripken. When
the Orioles were getting ready to leave for a road trip, traffic delayed
Ripken en route to the local airport. Ripken called team officials and
said he'd be there in 10 minutes. But Wren instructed the plane to take
off without Ripken, who did arrive at the gate just a few minutes later.
He wound up having to make his own way to Anaheim as the Orioles
headed west to play the Angels.

That incident clearly angered Oriole team officials, who took the
interesting step of addressing it when firing Wren shortly thereafter. In

Out of respect for his father, Ripken wears the No. 7 on his right sleeve. *(Photo by Stuart Zolotorow)*

the press release that announced Wren's removal, the team said: "In the opinion of management, there was no need for such an arbitrary and inflexible decision. In the meeting, Wren defiantly dismissed our concerns, characterized them as 'silly' and insisted he would invoke the same takeoff order no matter what the extenuating circumstances. The Orioles management cannot and will not abide having a GM operate in such an unreasonable, authoritarian manner and treat anyone this way, especially someone such as Cal who has done so much for the Orioles and for baseball."

Brady Anderson became one of Ripken's closest friends in baseball and was a popular figure during his long career with the Orioles. Anderson could be a jokester and had a great sense of humor that most people enjoyed. Ripken joined Anderson at Oriole Park when Anderson was inducted into the Oriole Hall of Fame in 2004.

Anderson also talked to reporters the night of Ripken's final game. He spoke about how Cal's retirement would affect so many people simply because they looked up to this man for what he did both on the baseball field and off of it.

"It's just interesting to think how he has possibly changed people's lives because of the way he conducts his life," Anderson said that day. "It's odd to have a player who's able to see how appreciated he is while he's still playing. A lot of people's careers end in untimely ways and they are forced into retirement, like Willie Mays for instance, who really struggled at the end. This is probably a retirement like no other in the history of baseball."

Anderson said that Ripken's popularity started, of course, with his ability. Ripken obviously became well known as an All-Star shortstop, and his fame grew when the Streak took on a life of its own. But there was more to Ripken's popularity.

"To reach the status that Cal has, there are a bunch of other factors. His integrity, his honesty ... I'm sure you've all interviewed him and maybe it is difficult to get to him at times, but I think that's because he is extremely intelligent and he would never give anyone an answer just to get rid of them," Anderson said that night. "He'll take his time and think about it. I think that if people really knew him, he'd be appreciated even more. There's a certain persona that people have which really isn't the real person. I would say the real person is better in this case."

The respect people have for Ripken and the way he treats them shows up all the time, even now, six years after his baseball career has ended.

Bill Stetka, now in charge of the Orioles media and public relations department, knows Ripken in many ways. He grew up in Bel Air, near Aberdeen, and went to school with one of Ripken's cousins. Stetka watched his brother, Joe, play baseball against Cal in high school.

"I covered Cal in the beginning as a back-up beat writer at the *News-American*. I saw him from a reporter aspect. I saw him as an official scorer, and then doing public relations for the club," Stetka said. "Reporting-wise, there were so many other players on those teams in the early '80s. In many ways, even though you knew Cal was a great ballplayer, you never kind of viewed him as a go-to guy. He was still kind of getting his feet wet. I probably first got to really know him when I was official scorer. I was working at Towson University, the *News-American* had folded, so I took over as official scorer in 1986. So, kind of, through the heart of the Streak as well as some of the fielding streaks he had, I [was there].

"It always interested me at times, the statistical freaks; [they] didn't regard him, you know, he didn't win any Gold Gloves. He had the one Gold Glove, but I mean, for so long he went without a Gold Glove, and people saw him as such an anomaly as shortstop because of his size. You had people like Bill James who didn't regard him as an outstanding shortstop, but until you watched him every day and saw where he played, you don't realize how good he is. Bill James wrote at one point, in 1991 I guess it was, when Cal had three errors and set a record for shortstops and James' book came out at the end of that season, ... something to the effect that 'Cal is not an outstanding shortstop. He's an average shortstop. The only reason he doesn't get errors is because the official scorer at Memorial Stadium won't call errors on him.' Well, I went back through and looked through the record book and saw that year I called two errors on him and he had one error on the road.

"There are certain things ... numbers can tell you certain things. Cal positioned himself so well. In calling a couple of errors on him, other players would complain to me and say, 'That shouldn't have been an error on Cal.' And if I went to Cal about it, he'd say, 'Well, I don't necessarily think it should have been. I think it was a tough play. If you think it's an error, so be it.'

"He never really complained about an error that was called on him, and if I went to him about something or a situation, it was always interesting to talk to him about not necessarily a situation involving him, but just ... examples of plays. If you were standing in the clubhouse and watching a play on the monitor and just chatting with him...you [would] see that. He could tell you certain things about how the guy maybe could have played it better or should have played it that really opened your eyes a lot more.

"So those were things that I always took out of the conversations with him. It may not have affected that call, but it basically opened my eyes up to other things down the road, and not just about shortstop. Cal could analyze any position on the field, about where a guy should be. That was the thing about Cal. They said he didn't have range, but he knew where to play. ..."

Stetka also talked about something many others discussed—the fact that Ripken could have sat more at various points to end the Streak. Having watched more Oriole games than most people ever will, he believed it to be a very simple situation.

"People have made the argument that his average might have been 10 to 15 points higher had he taken a day off every once in a while," Stetka said. "He could have sat some days when he was tired. He could have sat against the Randy Johnsons of the world, the Curt Schillings, the tough pitchers. But who else are you going to put out there? Do you have a better chance with Cal out there or the back-up middle infielder?"

A lot of the respect Ripken earned throughout the years showed up in the final seasons of his career. That's when the injuries began taking their toll—after he ended the Streak late in the 1998 season. He played in only 86 games in 1999 and just 83 the following year, the fewest of his career. Back problems hurt him again in 2000 when he was out over two months with inflammation in his lower back. Ripken then broke a rib in the spring of 2001, possibly while playing basketball before the season.

In an article that Ripken wrote in *The Baltimore Sun* on the 10th anniversary of his record-breaking moment, he discussed his thoughts about simply wanting to play on a regular basis and how he truly wanted nothing more than that.

"Remembering Dad being there always makes me recall how the [Streak] came to be," Ripken wrote. "It really was a lot simpler than people thought. I never set out to break any record or play in all of those games in a row. It was more of an approach. Dad always taught me that it is my job to show up to the ballpark every day prepared and ready to play and if the manager thinks you are one of the nine guys who can help the team win that day, you do the best you can. So if you think about it, managers like Earl Weaver, Joe Altobelli, and Frank Robinson were really responsible for the Streak. I just showed up, ready to play.

"Looking back, I remember how Frank Robinson once responded to a question about me and the Streak. He simply said that he wished he had 24 other guys who he could count on to be there every day.

Prior to a regular-season game, Ripken stands in the field for the pledge. *(Photo by Stuart Zolotorow)*

Frank always understood that the game is more than just hitting and fielding. There are many other ways to contribute on a daily basis. In the end, it is all about pulling together to try to win the game that day.

"It was always curious to me that there were times when I would have to defend my desire to play every day. Every once in a while a member of the media would say that I was selfish and that I was hurting the team. I never understood why the player who comes up with a mysterious injury so he wouldn't have to face Randy Johnson or Roger Clemens wasn't asked to defend himself. The Streak was really about an approach to the game that I learned from my dad, an approach that I always considered pure and honest."

John Valentin played many games against Ripken with the Boston Red Sox, and was another individual who loved watching how Cal did his job on a daily basis.

"As a player, obviously being a player, I had my work to do every day. I had to come out every day and do my job," Valentin said. "More than anything, from a player's point of view, watching him and knowing that he was going to be out there every day, that inspiration from a player to player from the preparation point of view, it made you go out there and make sure you were going to do your job as well. From a competitive standpoint and from a preparation standpoint, you knew he was going to be out there, so you'd try your best to be out there as well. He was definitely a smart player. He played a long time. He was a captain on the infield. He's a guy who can read the opposition's player, their strengths and their weaknesses, and know what the strengths and weaknesses of his pitching staff or the pitcher that was pitching that day and what they could do whether they could hit their spots, whether they could miss their spots, and he could be in the right place at the right time. More than anything, you noticed his consistency and his work ethic. Obviously, he is a Hall of Famer and he's going to be remembered for the games he played and his streak, obviously to be out there, the Iron Man, but he was still a workhorse.

Character

I'm sure there were many days he didn't want to be out there and he went there. What an influence that had to be with guys who played with him on the same team."

In the end, his character meant so much to those who knew, played, and worked with him. Despite all the surprising criticism he received about the Streak, no one questioned his work ethic. In the end, as complex as things grew with the Streak, everyone knew that there was just one thing behind it—Ripken just wanted to play.

14

MOMENTS TO REMEMBER

O ne of the curious things during Ripken's career was his ability to be involved with the right plays at just the right time, or other dramatic events that caught everyone's attention.

The moment most fans remember is that which happened over the two-night stretch in 1995 when Ripken tied and then broke Gehrig's mark. As baseball fans everywhere know, Ripken homered both nights in wins over the Angels. He then gave Baltimore fans one of their most emotional moments ever as he ad-libbed a run around the Oriole Park at Camden Yards warning track and shook hands with dozens of fans who just wanted to say thanks.

The Orioles were long out of the pennant race at that point and first-year manager Phil Regan was on his way out of town, but the world was watching on those two nights, and Ripken came through once more. Ripken had shown that propensity for creating drama throughout his career.

During the 1983 season, Ripken struggled at the plate when the Orioles went to the World Series. Despite winning in five games, most of the Orioles had problems hitting, and even though Ripken went just 3-for-18, he got a key RBI single in Game 2, a 4-1 Baltimore victory. The Orioles needed that game because the Phillies had taken

Baseball's Iron Man: Cal Ripken Jr., A Tribute

Game 1, and Baltimore didn't want to go to Philadelphia for its three-game stretch down two games to none.

And when Scott McGregor threw a complete game in the Series clincher, a 5-0 Baltimore victory, guess who made the final out? Ripken caught a soft liner off the bat of Garry Maddox to give the Orioles the title. Such moments just kept coming up throughout Ripken's career.

In 1988, when the Orioles made everyone in baseball laugh by losing 21 straight at the start of the season, Ripken had a big night as they finally ended the skid. He went 4-for-5 with a homer and a double in a 9-0 rout of the White Sox. He singled and scored on Eddie Murray's homer in the first to score the winning run.

His big moment in 1989 came on an Opening Day homer off Clemens. The three-run shot helped the Orioles rally for the 5-4 extra-innings victory but gave the young team a spark that lasted the entire season.

Ripken did it again in 1991 when he won the American League Most Valuable Player award, coming up big in the All-Star Game. One night after hitting 12 homers in the Home Run Derby, Ripken's three-run homer catapulted the American League to a win in the Mid-Summer Classic.

Ripken also wound up getting the final at-bat at Memorial Stadium. He came up with one out in the bottom of the ninth inning against Detroit starter Frank Tanana. The Tigers had taken an early lead that day and had rolled to a 7-1 lead when Ripken came up. He grounded into a double play that ended the game, the season, and the life of Memorial Stadium. Another batter would have had the chance had he reached base or just made an out, but the spotlight instead shined on Cal once more.

One of the most memorable moments of Ripken's career came in his final year. Ripken had announced his retirement in June of 2001, and he was clearly struggling. He was on the All-Star team, but had

As Baltimore honors the rescue workers of September 11, Ripken looks toward the flag. *(Photo by Mike Theiler/AFP/Getty Images)*

only a .240 batting average with four homers and 28 RBIs, numbers far lower than had been his norm throughout his career.

But that evening in Seattle turned out to be a memorable one for Ripken's fans when everything came together.

Ripken, of course, had played third base for the last few seasons, but when he went out to third base in the first inning, he saw Alex Rodriguez already there. The young superstar pointed at Ripken to go to shortstop. Cal didn't get it at first before Rodriguez laughed and gently pushed him over toward the position.

The message—go back to shortstop for a while.

American League manager Joe Torre and Rodriguez wanted Ripken to spend some time in his final All-Star Game at the position for which he was best known—shortstop. Ripken even made a play there before going back to third base in the second inning.

"I must have been the only one on the whole planet that didn't know," Ripken said to reporters that night. "I went out there and thought about it—this isn't the time or place to go back to short. I haven't played it in so many years. [Alex] said, 'No, everybody is expecting you to do it, so go on over there.'"

Things got even better when Ripken came to bat for the first time in the third inning. The Seattle crowd gave him a long standing ovation, and Ripken got more cheers when he lined Chan Ho Park's first pitch over the left-field fence for a homer.

That homer was Ripken's second in All-Star competition, but it gave chills to so many people. He just seemed to keep finding ways to do things under pressure. The American League won the game 4-1, but not many people were that interested. What Ripken did had stolen the spotlight once more as he earned game MVP honors.

"I had a shot of adrenaline or a long case of the goose bumps, I'm not sure yet," Ripken said that night. "But coming to the plate, I was excited. I was a little worried with the shadows. I went up there and said, 'God, it's hard to see. Let me just keep things short and put the ball in play.'"

Torre and some players later talked about Ripken and how they wanted to pay tribute to him.

"This whole Cal Ripken thing, and here I am thinking of making changes," Torre told reporters afterwards. "And bang, somebody is saying get up, get up, and he hit a home run. It was really magical. And Cal is such, he's such a class individual, and his legacy in baseball is just going to be not how he played, but the way he played, the way he carried himself."

Derek Jeter and Sammy Sosa both offered similar thoughts after the game.

"I don't see how he does it," Jeter said. "He always seems to come up with home runs on his big days. He tied the streak, he broke the streak, he hit home runs. I think someone mentioned before the game, 'Watch, Cal is going to be the MVP of this game.' He did it again."

Said Sosa: "Wow, it's like a dream come true, especially, you know, everybody was on his feet and clapping and after that, he came in with the home run. It doesn't get any better than that as a human being. That's a great feeling, especially [because] he announced his retirement and came and put up a shot like that. That's amazing. He is the man. He is the man."

It was almost mystical how Ripken managed to do it. Former Oriole great Brooks Robinson had a similar ability. He hit a big home run when he hit his 200th homer and kept making big plays in places like the World Series. Ripken did the same thing—over and over again.

In fact, what most people outside of Baltimore probably remember about the back-to-back celebration the nights that Ripken tied and broke the Gehrig record are Cal's home runs. Would it have changed much if Ripken went 0-for-4 on both nights? Probably not, since the

Orioles weren't contending for anything. But coming up with such big hits just added to the legend.

15

LOOKING BACK ON THE RECORD

The Orioles and Ripken celebrated on consecutive nights in 2005—the 10th anniversary of Cal's record-breaking moment. The first part of the celebration came September 5 at Ripken Stadium prior to an Aberdeen IronBirds game, and the second part came the following night at Oriole Park. The difference between the two ceremonies show what Ripken is all about.

The first night looked like a small gathering of friends, when many from Aberdeen and the surrounding area greeted and talked to Ripken before the ceremony. Murray came back to town to help honor his old friend. He wouldn't come the following night because of his anger toward the Orioles over his treatment, nor would he speak with the media again, with one exception. As he walked past the IronBirds dugout after Ripken had just finished talking to reporters, one of the writers asked, "Can you believe it's been 10 years, Eddie?"

Murray smiled and kept walking before he turned around.

"Time flies," he said.

That first night was not the type of big-time celebration one would expect. It was more like a small, quiet party for a bunch of local folks. There weren't suits and ties. It wasn't terribly formal. Fans were loose and relaxed, and so was Ripken. He wore a blue IronBirds shirt and

Baseball's Iron Man: Cal Ripken Jr., A Tribute

Eddie Murray joins Ripken for the record-breaking anniversary festivities in 2005.
(*Photo by Stuart Zolotorow*)

black dress pants that night. There was a small pregame ceremony on the infield, where Ripken talked to the crowd, thanked them, and told a few jokes. It sounded like a real family gathering.

Even Murray got involved. He came out wearing a smooth tan outfit that looked like it had come from the '70s or '80s. The crowd quickly got into the celebration once they saw him. The familiar chant of "Ed-die, Ed-die" that rocked Memorial Stadium, and later Oriole Park, began very quickly. Murray noticed it, smiled, and waved to the crowd. Ripken and Murray then reunited to start the game. Ripken went out to the mound, laughing and motioning for Murray, who was standing at home plate, to go into a catcher's crouch. Murray, also laughing, followed orders. Ripken threw a strike from the mound and the crowd of about 6,000—a sell-out—erupted.

Looking Back on the Record

Even the meeting with the press before the game remained low-key. Ripken and his teenage daughter, Rachel, came into the dugout before the game and sat down on the hot late-summer night. The Aberdeen players watched with curiosity while pretending to warm up as Ripken talked quietly to the media.

He addressed everyone, even those from small papers or radio stations, answering the questions he'd heard so many times before. "For the most part, my career went by like that, and 2,131, looking back, seems like just yesterday," Ripken said.

Ripken enjoyed looking back on the Streak and the night he broke the record, because it became so big and so much fun. He also said it was great to have Murray present, because he always credited the first baseman as contributing a big part to his success. Murray was one of the older players who took Ripken under his wing in the early days, especially when he struggled so much at first. He pushed him along the right path and kept him focused.

"It's a nice opportunity to reflect," Ripken said, sitting in the IronBirds dugout before the game. "It's always good to go back. It makes you feel warm and fuzzy."

However, one question came up that truly made Ripken laugh. Everyone remembered Ripken's victory lap around the field at Oriole Park on the night he broke the record. It was a moment that everyone would agree is among the most memorable in team history. It was a moment that was born out of sheer emotion and happiness. It was a moment that touched many people.

"At first I was very self-conscious about holding up the game," Ripken said. "I didn't think it was right, but as I made my way around the field it went from a big celebration to a very personal one. I saw people I knew and faces I recognized. By the time I got around to the Angels dugout I couldn't care less if [the game] ever started again. The entire night was incredible. I would say my greatest memory was waving to my dad. He was in the suite and we saw each other and just waved to each other. It was a very powerful moment."

But when asked if he'd take another victory lap, Ripken laughed. "I hope not," he said.

The celebration at Oriole Park the following night was a bit bigger and filled with emotion. The Orioles, as in 1995, were in the final days of a disappointing season. They had been in first place for a long time, surprising the world, before falling apart after the All-Star Break. Now they were just playing out the string, and this night gave them a chance to remember a big moment.

They brought the famous warehouse numbers out once more, replaying the ceremony and unfurling "2,131" across the wall to once more delight the fans. The Orioles again brought Ripken onto the field, and he earned yet another standing ovation.

Ripken looked like a businessman this time, wearing a dark suit and shirt, but still appeared ready to play. After the ovation, his fans pushed him to take another lap. But he emphatically shook his head. No, guys, not this time. He smiled and walked off the field behind home plate.

"It was just a wonderful experience," Ripken said of the night 10 years ago. "I fulfilled a dream. I wish I could play for another 3,000 games."

The Orioles had a little fun with present-day shortstop Miguel Tejada to illustrate the enormity of what Ripken accomplished. At that time, Tejada had the longest consecutive-games streak among active players. He had played in 894 straight games, and the Orioles informed Tejada that he really could catch Ripken if he continued to play in every game.

It just wouldn't happen until July of 2016.

Ripken came upstairs after the event and talked with reporters in a room across from the media dining room above the press box. He spoke for several minutes, joked all the time, yet answered the

Ripken, signing autographs in 2005, clearly hasn't forgotten about the fans.
(Photo by Stuart Zolotorow)

questions, "I'm still pretty amazed," Ripken said. "I think everyone, in [some] way, wants to leave a mark. It's OK if people remember [that]."

But the biggest memory for most people either present or watching on television in 1995 was the lap around the field. "It had a huge impact on me," Ripken said. "It was very spontaneous. I felt a little ridiculous [at first]. There's no way somebody could've planned that. That was a great experience. It was wonderful to go through. There was genuine excitement."

J.T. Snow, who played on the Angels that night, still had appreciation for the record 10 years later. He said that players get hurt and sick constantly, but Ripken was able to keep everything going for such a long time—something that doesn't happen as much any more.

"I think it's the most remarkable thing I've seen in my career as far as milestones go," Snow said. "That's a record nobody thought would be broken. Guys make break home-run records or hitting streaks, but to play 2,400-2,500 games in a row was amazing."

In the end, that's what Ripken and his friends and family celebrated both nights on his record-breaking 10th anniversary. He always was proud of just playing the game because he was doing his job, nothing else. Breaking a big home run or batting record is one thing, but this was about living up to the values his parents instilled in him. Come to work, do your job, and live up to your obligations to the team. It's a memory Ripken will always be glad to have.

"Here's to September 6, here's to Camden Yards, and here's to all of you," Ripken told the crowd in 2005, drawing yet another standing ovation.

16

THE NEW GAME

"It was a little bit of an accident," Ripken said with a smile last summer. "I had planned to move in the direction of youth baseball at the end of my career … in 1995, as a gift for breaking the record, the Players Association gave me a $75,000 grant to go back and build a "Field of Dreams" in my hometown. When I looked at it, I thought, what a great concept … but $75,000 doesn't go very far to put into a field, so I was going to put my money into it and try to figure out a way to get four or five fields out of this so [we'd] have a nice complex here in the community."

And so the Aberdeen Project came to life. Bringing the IronBirds to Aberdeen proved to be the first step. Ripken connected with Peter Kirk, who has owned and run minor-league franchises in the Mid-Atlantic area for several years.

"They were looking for a minor-league team at the same time under Peter Kirk, and so we were bumping into each other for parcels of land and where to put these different complexes or places, and Peter Kirk needed some help going into the Governor's office to get support from the state," Ripken said. "I was that person, so we formed a partnership, and that's how I got into the minor-league baseball side."

Ripken said that, as they moved along, it became a public-private partnership between the city of Aberdeen, Harford County, and the state of Maryland. The state itself came in at a third of the cost of building the minor-league stadium, the city and county added a third, and Kirk and Ripken did the same.

But that's when things changed a bit.

The entire process seemed to be dragging for a while as they got the deal to a certain point of sponsorship and ticket sales to keep the risk as low as possible.

"It's kind of funny, my mom came to me and asked me what was going on, were we ever going to put a shovel in the ground," Ripken said, with a laugh. "So I went back to Peter Kirk and said, 'You know, let's get moving on this.' And he said at this point in his life, he's not willing to take that sort of risk, so I assumed the whole thing. Peter Kirk's idea then was more of an independent team. When I came into the project, I was affiliated and I wanted an affiliated team. And so we were moving forward. So I reached out to see how I could find a team and bring a team in here. That's how the minor-league thing started, and I worked like crazy."

Ripken said that once events began taking place, everything seemed to keep rolling faster and faster. He didn't have much time to relax after taking off his Oriole uniform for the final time in the fall of 2001. He actually began meetings to bring a new team to Aberdeen almost immediately afterward—and the IronBirds began play in June 2002.

"As soon as I retired, I ended up taking a jersey off and putting a suit on, buying the team and [jumping] through all the different territorial issues that were [there]," Ripken said. "To get that done … it was what you had to do, but it seemed pretty miraculous, looking back on the time frame. But again, it was all under the wanting to do good stuff and wanting to bring back to the community and do what's right for baseball. That was a wonderful thing. That became our focus. That was the first piece. It all seemed to start falling into place."

Ripken said that USA Baseball was looking to move at that time, so his company tossed its hat into the ring and drew some serious interest. Even though they lost—USA Baseball now is based in Durham, North Carolina—the experience taught Ripken and his company some important lessons.

"We tried to get USA Baseball, who was moving their complex from Arizona, and ... we were competing with cities like Atlanta, Jupiter, and Raleigh ... so I called up the governor again and I said, 'I think this is a good idea. What do you think?' The governor [said], 'I think it's a great idea to bring USA Baseball to the state of Maryland.' I said, 'Well, I don't know how to do it.' So he gave me his chief of his staff and started directing me on how to put together a value proposition for USA Baseball," said Ripken. "We ended up losing, but we ... [looked] at our complex and [looked] at pieces of property that were now available. We master planned it. ... So it had an added benefit, the exercise we went through. It ultimately attracted a developer to the area."

That's one of the things that helped the entire complex grow into, well, a complex. But Ripken Stadium came first. Home to the Aberdeen IronBirds, the $18-million stadium opened in 2002. The team plays in the New York-Penn League and has become a Class A affiliate of the Orioles. The year before, Harford County had hosted an independent team that didn't fare too well in attendance. Ripken's business felt that connecting the team to the Orioles also was important in order to gain local fan support.

"...We were building the stadium when [Ripken] retired, and there was no team and there was a real risk there," said Maroon. "[He] had to go to [Orioles owner Peter] Angelos and say, 'Look, if I get a team will you add an affiliate?' He jumped into that right away, and it turned out to be the best move ever. ..."

When the group worked out everything involving the stadium, the affiliation, and the team, the IronBirds literally took off. Finding an IronBirds ticket is nearly an impossible task. The games are often sold out even before the 38-game home season begins in mid-June. The team gets great local media coverage in Harford County and has become an important part of Ripken's hometown. Many in the area were grateful that Ripken picked Aberdeen to do his business. It became very popular almost immediately and helped the town fiscally.

"The fact that he chose to come back to Harford County and put his money here is great," Morrison said. "He could have put his money anywhere. [The IronBirds] have 38 games in June through early September, and it is just remarkable, and I told his mom that. He is an astute man who has an unerring sense of what's right. ..."

Aberdeen itself doesn't have a huge metropolis of fans to draw from. It's about 25 miles south of the Delaware state line, and the city of Baltimore is about 35 minutes away—on a good day, or if the traffic keeps moving. But the minor-league team has sold out every game for all five years of its existence. In fact, trying to find an IronBirds ticket can be even tougher than trying to find one for the Baltimore Ravens.

The *Baltimore Business Journal* reported in an article last summer that there are about 1,400 people on a waiting list for season tickets to see the IronBirds at Ripken Stadium. Even more impressive is the fact that this baseball team is at one of the lowest levels in the minor leagues. Their season runs from about mid-June till the first week in September, two months shorter than the minor leagues above them.

In the same article, team vice president Jeff Eiseman said the IronBirds drew 75 percent of its crowds from Harford County, which is impressive. Morrison agreed with many others that Ripken's involvement is very valuable to the team's success.

"No one else could have come to Aberdeen and made happen what has happened there in such a short time," Morrison said. "When

Home of the Aberdeen IronBirds, Ripken Stadium opened in 2002. *(Photo by Stuart Zolotorow)*

you look at what it has spawned, it's amazing. It has changed the image of Aberdeen, and it's a positive image. ..."

The Ripken name can only take things so far, but the 6,100-seat stadium also sits a long fly ball from I-95 and is easily seen by anyone driving it.

"It's definitely one of the finer stadiums in the league," said New York-Penn League President Ben Hayes within the article. "They are not blessed with a market such as Brooklyn or Staten Island, where millions of fans live such a short distance away. They are constantly reviewing their ticket packages and trying to craft packages that are appealing to the fans and something the fans would want."

Ripken Baseball started in 2001, and its mission was to help the game of baseball grow throughout the world and be taught the right way. After Cal retired from the Orioles, Ripken Baseball expanded into four areas: Ripken Management and Design, Youth Camps and Clinics, the Cal Ripken Sr. Foundation, and the IronBirds. A new division, IronClad Authentics, started last year to supervise the company's corporate licensing, manage Ripken's signature, and develop an Internet retail store, www.ironcladauthentics.com.

Ripken isn't the type of owner to interfere with things every day. He keeps a low profile. Although Ripken talks to young players on occasion, he often just walks through the stands and converses with people. He comes to the Ripken Baseball office every day to deal with things that need to be dealt with—and enjoys doing it.

Jay Moskowitz handled public relations with the IronBirds for two seasons before moving up to work in marketing for Ripken Baseball, and says Ripken is just like any other businessperson.

"Cal likes things [to be] done the right way, and that's what should be expected of any company that you'd run," Moskowitz said. "He's more of an idea person and doesn't mind giving things out to people to get them done. He thinks big picture. He uses the vehicle of baseball to try and advance the other things that are important to him in life, like teaching kids and growing through the game of baseball and giving kids the life lessons through sports, in a nutshell. That's the aim of the company—it's perpetuating what's important to them through the use of baseball."

Ripken wants to add more minor-league teams to his portfolio, and company officials have said he'd like to look at purchasing one a year for the next 10 years, if that's possible. He started moving toward this goal in June of 2005, when Ripken Professional Baseball bought the Augusta GreenJackets from the HWS Baseball Group. The team plays in the Class A South Atlantic League—the same league as that of the Delmarva Shorebirds, a Baltimore affiliate. Augusta is actually a San Francisco Giants affiliate.

Ripken also faced an interesting, if unusual, situation when the Washington Nationals moved to the nation's capital from Montreal after the 2004 season. Major League Baseball owned the team and took longer than expected in naming an ownership group. In fact, it wasn't until early in 2006 that the Lerner family was awarded the team. But Ripken had a good chance to get involved.

"The Washington ownership groups came hard at him," Maroon said. "He appreciated it, and he met with them, heard what they had to say before they got the ownership [issue settled]. He was very flattered, very intrigued by that, but said, 'I'm a Baltimore guy.'"

Maroon thought for a moment and smiled when asked what he thought Ripken would really like to do if he had the chance in baseball.

"My opinion is, I think he'd love to buy the Orioles," Maroon said. "I think that would be his ultimate dream."

17

POST-PLAYING CAREER: A CLOSER LOOK

The outdoor lunch held to help kick off the 2006 Cal Ripken World Series on a very hot and humid Sunday last August kept everyone scurrying around. From the volunteers helping teams find their way to those serving food to players, coaches, and umpires to the people taking tickets, everyone seemed to be talking about what the upcoming week would bring.

Children who had come to the quiet town of Aberdeen, Maryland, about 30 to 35 miles north of Oriole Park at Camden Yards, were wandering around in their game uniforms and talking to teammates. Players from different teams often got together to talk—when possible, since a number of teams came from other countries like Mexico, the Dominican Republic, and Korea, and were still working on their command of the English language.

This is a common occurrence at the Ripken World Series: children from all over the world brought together by baseball. All games were once held at Ripken Stadium, the facility the former Oriole great built to house the Aberdeen IronBirds, but as Ripken's vision for what he could do for youth baseball began to take shape, the concept expanded.

Instead of playing only at Ripken Stadium, the children now use other fields at the Ripken Youth Academy, including Cal Sr.'s Yard, which is owned and operated by the Cal Ripken Sr. Foundation, a non-profit organization that works to provide baseball and softball programs for underprivileged kids. A hotel is presently being built behind the right-field wall of Cal Sr.'s Yard to give it a look amazingly similar to Oriole Park at Camden Yards. The kids also play on a field with a 24-foot green wall that makes some feel like they are in Boston at Fenway Park. Fields have also been built to remind children of Wrigley Field in Chicago and Memorial Stadium, the Orioles' home from 1954 to 1991.

This is all part of Ripken's vision for a place unlike any other to teach children baseball. The Ripken World Series continues to grow every year and keeps drawing bigger television coverage. The Babe Ruth League, Inc., helped the Ripken World Series by renaming its youth baseball division for kids 12 and under. Once the Bambino Division, it is now called the Cal Ripken Baseball Division, and has begun to lay the groundwork for the Little League World Series.

The World Series is becoming more popular for a number of reasons. It has been a fixture in Williamsport, Pennsylvania, for a long time, and Babe Ruth Baseball never quite broke through onto the national stage, especially when it involved media coverage. ABC and ESPN have long televised the Little League World Series, but FOX quickly picked up the Ripken Series.

Ripken and his brother, Bill, are two of the reasons the series has grown so popular. Teams who play come from all over the world and are given plenty of chances to meet the Ripkens and talk baseball. During the 2004 Ripken World Series, both men sat out talking and answering all kinds of players' questions around 10:30 p.m. on a Friday night. There were no cameras or media. Cal and Bill simply spoke with a bunch of kids sitting in Little League uniforms. Coaches also attended and enjoyed the experience as much as the children.

Post-Playing Career: A Closer Look

The IronBirds' stadium is located right next door to Cal Sr.'s Yard. During his Ripken World Series, Cal mentioned how much he loved that children who play in his tournament can just walk right over to watch the New York-Penn League All-Star Game on any given night.

Listening to what his father used to say about how to get a job done remains the driving force in Ripken's dreams and goals—and probably will be for a long time.

"We go back to what Dad used to say to us a thousand times: 'If it's worth doing, it's worth doing right—otherwise, don't do it at all,'" Ripken said. "What he was talking about is there's an emphasis on quality, there's an emphasis on doing it not halfway but all the way through. Hopefully, everything we put our effort into is going to be to that vision that says, 'If it's worth doing, it's worth doing right,' and we'll go to the nth degree to make sure it's done in a quality fashion."

Ripken takes great pride in the fact that he's built a baseball complex that can both help children and serve a community. Everything is coming together in a way that makes Ripken very happy and should help the Harford County area grow in the coming months and years.

"The hotel became a reality; the avenue concept of the movie theater ... it's become a reality," Ripken said. "We enhanced our design of our little guys' complex because we hooked up big fields and small fields in conjunction with each other. So then it really came together once we really started pushing the tournament [members] and...our camping through there. The last few years have been very successful in those areas. The minor-league baseball business was a little bit by accident. My intention and my passion [were] on the kids' side. But minor-league baseball experience, I've discovered, is absolutely ... the thing that I needed the most in my transition from playing baseball to business, because ... it's a real service-oriented business, it's a community gathering place. [There are] a lot of lessons to be learned, and it really works."

Ripken is passionate about making the children's facility something that's different and special. Children can play in any kind of tournament on any kind of field, but Ripken wants something unusual, mainly to let them enjoy the game he loves and his father loved teaching.

"On the kids' side over there ... we wanted to make sure the fields were big-league-caliber, quality fields," Ripken said. "We value that. Not that we're looking at it as a business niche. We want to breathe life and fresh air into youth baseball by teaching it, but also by matching the facilities with the experience. The same feeling I had walking into Camden Yards or walking into Memorial Stadium or walking into Fenway or Yankee Stadium ... as a professional player, that's one of the greatest feelings in the world to compete in that environment, realizing that only a few people understand what that feeling's like. I wanted to bring that feeling down to the 12-year-olds, to the young guys. And that's really part of the mission. We're a stickler on maintaining our fields and ... you can almost boast that our Fenway over there might be in better condition to field ground balls off of than the real Fenway, and the same is true for Camden Yards. Camden Yards is a beautiful field and they maintain it really well, but I would say that ours is comparable, or as good or better than theirs. I want the kids to leave here and say, 'That was a great baseball experience, that was the greatest field I've ever played on.' If you can get to that point, you know you've reached them in ways, in depths, that [don't] translate just from learning how to play baseball, pitching, and hitting and all that kind of stuff. You've gone deeper into the experience."

Ripken Baseball's goal is to work with children and teach them "The Ripken Way." Ripken has now opened two baseball academies, one of which just started last summer with a number of baseball fields in Myrtle Beach, South Carolina. It's truly a passion for both Ripkens, who can always be seen working with the players throughout the various camps and instructional programs.

Last summer, the Ripken facility was also to serve as the official home of the Myrtle Beach National Adult Baseball Association (NABA). The league was scheduled to have four teams with semi-professional players. Games were set for 11 different dates, from June through August. This association is made up of players at least 18 years old and takes place in 34 different states throughout the United States.

In Myrtle Beach, the "Ripken Experience" is set to feature six youth and three regulation-size baseball fields, each one modeled after one of baseball's historic parks, including places like the Polo Grounds, US Cellular Field, and Forbes Field.

The Ripkens have also worked at getting their message out in print with a book called *Play Baseball the Ripken Way: The Complete Illustrated Guide to the Fundamentals.* The book sold well and got good reviews. *Publishers Weekly* said the book is "the next best thing to a personal lesson with the man who broke Lou Gehrig's record of playing in 2,632 consecutive games; it's a comprehensive look at all aspects of how to play baseball that will benefit young players and adult weekend warriors. ..."

Ripken's seemingly never-ending passion for the game and its details doesn't surprise those who've known him for long periods of time.

Ernie Tyler is known as the "baseball guy" at Oriole Park and—before that—Memorial Stadium. Since 1960, the public has seen Tyler as the man who runs out and hands the home plate umpire baseballs when needed. Like Ripken and his father before him, Tyler is a Harford County guy. Talking about Jr. today brings a smile to Tyler's face.

"He's never changed. I see him over at Ripken Stadium, and he's just like you," Tyler said. "You talk to people, and it's not a matter of you talking to an icon, it's just that's what he is. Consider what he's done up at Aberdeen. Someday it's going to be matched with Disneyland because he's got so much going up there. He's the same as he was when he was 14, 15, or 20. He's a local kid, and his father was in baseball. I don't think that adds to his popularity."

Tyler strongly believes that Ripken adds to his own popularity by the way he behaves. Living in a world where many sports stars want everything given to them and are willing to give little, if anything, back, Ripken is something different.

Tyler agrees that Ripken has continued to be a small-town boy at heart. He remains polite to everyone, looks people right in the eye when talking, and never plays the star routine.

"Sometimes he'll be out here sitting in his seat when [coming to Oriole Park], and I walk over and say hi, he'll put his finger through the screen and shake," Tyler said. "You don't have to do that. That's just the way he acts. He [was] that way all the way through his career."

Andy Etchebarren is another person who's known Ripken for a long time. Etchebarren was the IronBirds manager in the 2005 and 2006 seasons. The long-time Oriole catcher played on a regular basis from 1966 to 1975. Etchebarren twice made the All-Star team and was part of the Orioles during their glory days, when they won four American League championships in six years (1966, 1969-71), along with two World Series titles (1966, 1970).

Etchebarren played for Ripken Sr. in Aberdeen, South Dakota, in 1963. Etchebarren said he's got some memories of the younger Ripken—who would have been pushing the age of three at that time—running around that ballpark in diapers. Etchebarren has enjoyed seeing what that little kid has grown into.

"He was in here the other day, and I talked to him," Etchebarren said late last summer before an IronBirds game. "I think he enjoys all those kids over there, having a nice facility, giving back to the community, number one. He was born here, raised here, his mom still lives here, he still lives here. I think he's done a wonderful job here. It's not going to get worse, it's going to get better. It's going to get bigger and better. This is going to be a wonderful place for kids to come. It's a wonderful situation."

Ripken said there's no question in his mind what his dad would think of this facility. In fact, when asked what his father's thoughts would be about it, Cal simply leaned back in a chair and laughed.

"I think Dad would be out of his mind," he said. "He might be arguing with us, thinking we're getting too big for our britches, trying to keep us humble and grounded, but I guarantee you he'd be on a tractor, he'd be behind a rake, he'd be teaching baseball, he'd have a fungo in his back pocket. He'd be out there in all … capacities day in and day out, from the first time [a] kid arrived here until … the last person left in the evening."

Ripken said that he has a feeling that his father's spirit is with him in some form.

"In the last few days … it almost feels like Dad is walking with us," Cal said during the middle of the Ripken World Series. "I can't really explain that any more than just a feeling. And when you're going around talking to kids or many times when you see Billy talking to kids, it's almost like Dad's speaking through Billy. It's the darned thing, it comes out, it looks just like Dad."

Looking back at everything, it's not surprising that Ripken ended up working in baseball even after retiring as a player. Why would he do anything else? His life revolved around his father's career as a child, he played for the team his dad worked for as an adult, and then became affiliated with that same ballclub when his playing time was finished.

Baseball played such a large role in Ripken's life that it's where he's been the most comfortable, even though the game now comes to him through a business perspective.

"My whole life was baseball. Dad was a player in the minor leagues … he was in the minor leagues for the first 14 years of my life," he said. "We traveled to where he was when we were out of school and

Cal Sr.'s Yard is one of many complexes that hosts the Cal Ripken World Series.
(Photo by Stuart Zolotorow)

spent the summers whenever he managed and we spent the days at the ballpark. I went to the ballpark with my dad each and every day. I worked as a batboy, shined shoes, worked in the clubhouse, ran errands to the concession stands, did all kinds of stuff, hung around baseball. In many ways, when we had life lessons or school lessons, Dad seemed to always explain things in terms of his baseball experiences. I tend to do the same thing. I try to understand things by putting [them] into a baseball incubator, and then try to spit [them] back out [into] … real-world problems."

18

WHAT THE
FUTURE HOLDS

M any people familiar with Cal Ripken Jr.—and Cal Ripken
Sr.—understand what baseball has always meant to the family.
The elder Ripken grew into a kind of baseball guru, especially within
the Orioles organization. During the Orioles' glory years, from the
mid-'60s to the mid-'80s, everyone in baseball knew about "The
Oriole Way."

Those who played "The Oriole Way" simply did everything in a
fundamentally sound style that emphasized good mechanics. If the
basics were handled correctly, a solid base was provided upon which a
player could learn how to do everything else. If a ball was hit to the
outfield, a player could try for a good throw home—but had to make
sure the ball could be cut off by an infielder just in case.

Cal Ripken Sr. was all about teaching and preaching those
concepts. So many Orioles who went on to become stars say they
learned "The Oriole Way" from him. Ask most any Oriole who played
in the farm system in the 1960s or '70s, and it's a good bet that the
elder Ripken taught them something. This is the tradition his son is
trying to carry on now.

When Cal Ripken Jr. describes his mission with Ripken Baseball,
it's easy to see what's on his mind.

"The whole vision of this place with kids I think came basically and directly from kids, " Ripken said. "Dad always cared about passing the craft of baseball on to kids, and he defined kids as people who were in minor league baseball and were in the Oriole organization that he taught and delivered messages to, and also the kids in his camps that he taught. You can see him talking to anybody but it seemed like the light would go off brighter when he was talking to kids, because it seemed to have a bigger effect. It [is] when something resonates with a kid you can instantly see that there's this confidence that grows, and that they want to try it more and they want to practice more. Dad was always very much [interested] in passing that on. … Specifically with me, I had a good influence with the kids. I remember how I felt toward players when I was growing up, and all of a sudden there were kids that were feeling like that about me. I wanted to continue what Dad had really enjoyed doing his whole life, but [do] it in a bigger way, affecting more kids. Dad really loved to keep it small, affect the kids that he could touch … I always thought Dad had this gift and this thing that he could pass on the craft to many more people, therefore impacting baseball in a more positive way. So I guess it's a combination of Dad's instruction, his fundamental way, his teaching way, and my desire to actually include the masses and enlarge it."

Teaching and working with kids has truly become a passion for Ripken. It's easy to see how much he enjoys being with children around the baseball field. In an age of diva-like stars, Ripken truly remains a small-town guy. Many in Harford County treat him with awe for several reasons, the biggest of which seems to be the fact that Ripken still loves spending time with their children. A child never needs to be afraid to come up to him to talk or ask baseball advice—he'll give it.

In a July 2006 interview with CNN, Ripken discussed the pressure that presently exists in children's sports. The era of the overzealous parent has blossomed in full force, and Ripken thinks that, as his

Ripken visits with a young patient at Johns Hopkins Children's Center. *(Photo by Stuart Zolotorow)*

father did, they have to toe that line between being supportive and over-supportive. Ripken also said children need to understand that not everything is going to be good in baseball, and the world won't end if someone makes an error in a game or if they strike out. This is something that can relieve pressure.

"Before kids really learn how to play, they need to experience the good and the bad, sometimes the positive, sometimes the negative, a little adversity, and they need to learn the game, and they should be allowed to make mistakes," he told CNN. "When you emphasize winning, those mistakes really aren't allowed. So, to me, the pressure has kind of trickled down. Maybe it's because the big-league game is so big now, the salaries are so big that parents want the best for their kids, and they want to give them the best chance possible. I think the intentions are good, but, to me, the atmosphere is way too pressurized for the kids to cope."

Ernie Tyler, the Orioles' other Iron Man, remembers watching Jr. in his younger days when he'd come to Memorial Stadium—the team's home until Oriole Park at Camden Yards opened in 1992—to work with his father on his game. Tyler understands why Ripken still has a love and a passion for the game that simply won't burn out. It's been a part of Ripken's life since his childhood.

"Little Cal would come to the ballpark, and the old man would hit him ground balls and it went on forever," Tyler said. "He started getting 100 foul balls a day, and then Cal shagged flies in the outfield. How much attention do you pay to a ballplayer or a coach or anybody else who brings a kid to the ballpark? You figure he's just trying to teach him. Cal brought his son down here. Ryan is good at second base and was hitting the ball [far and] was only seven years old then when I [saw him]. He's a left-handed hitter, and you [think] gee, he's going to be just like his dad, he's going to turn into something good if he likes the game like his dad and his grandfather did. It's a real close family, they're just like normal next-door neighbors."

Ripken himself likes the fact that he's building a mix—one that will help little kids as well as minor-league players. The aforementioned little league stadiums will sit in the same location as Ripken Stadium. A shopping facility is scheduled to be a long fly ball from both the adult and kids' baseball fields. It's an area that children and adults alike will love to visit for anything involving baseball.

Having the ability to build this model is tremendously satisfying to Ripken. He can carry on his father's dream in a much bigger way. He'll help more children learn, understand, and love the game of baseball.

Ripken's goal isn't to work with kids in order to develop miniature major-league players. Its just about introducing children to baseball

What The Future Holds

Located in Aberdeen, Ripken's hotel is just part of his plan to build up baseball.
(Photo by Stuart Zolotorow)

and letting them have fun, something that many people have lost sight of in this high-pressure world in which we live.

"We've built a very interesting model here," Ripken said. " I love the fact that minor-league baseball is played here where kids and families can come and watch and dream a little bit. And I also like the fact that right next door you can live out your dream, you can play it. I think that there's great synergy between a minor-league ballpark and a kids complex right next to each other. The hotel is still under construction. [There are] going to be so many people around the two events that you're going to see some crossover; you're going to see some people curious to see what the little guys are doing over there. Our World Series is totally free, it's wide open and you can go over there and see what's going on. There's a wonderful crossover between the two. But yes, looking at markets, our first look is we're trying to find a way to have a similar model that we built in Aberdeen here. In Augusta, we weren't able to do that, but there's an opportunity to build a small field in center field and kind of carry on the same sort of community gathering place. … We want the kids to play. We want to see kids play baseball. We like to use the stadium for the community. We like to have them feel like it's theirs. I'd like to try to duplicate it. If at all possible, I'd like to find ball teams that have an opportunity to have a youth complex right next door."

19

ENTERING THE HALL

The question made him pause for a second. He's obviously heard it many times before, but it seems like Cal Ripken Jr. is very careful when it comes to addressing the fact that he could very well be joining the Hall of Fame later this summer.

Ripken clearly has thought about it. Many in Baltimore and in the baseball world consider Ripken an obvious choice for the Hall of Fame, and think that his spot in Cooperstown has long been locked up. Talk of the Hall began during Ripken's Oriole career, when he established himself as one of the game's best shortstops, despite winning only two Gold Gloves. Interestingly, he won both of these honors at a time when most players slow down, midway through his career in 1991 and 1992.

Making the All-Star Game each year from 1983 to 2001, Ripken was the best-known Oriole in many seasons at a time when the franchise began to struggle. But breaking Lou Gehrig's consecutive-games record pushed his recognition factor even higher on the national level. Along with Joe DiMaggio's 56-game hitting streak, a mark that's stood on its own since 1941, Gehrig's record was one of very few considered to be unbreakable.

Baseball's Iron Man: Cal Ripken Jr., A Tribute

Ripken broke the Gehrig mark at the right time, just after a strike ended the 1994 season in August and cost the sport the playoffs and World Series. Fans were still angry the following year, but Ripken was able to get some five-star, positive coverage for baseball. People had already been talking about Ripken's possibility as a future Hall of Famer, and breaking the record seemed to lock that concept into place.

In fact, Ripken knows that people have spoken about it a great deal since he retired after the 2001 season. And he clearly is hoping to see it happen, but doesn't want to jump ahead of the game by talking about it too much. That's why he paused when asked about it during his World Series in Maryland last summer. It was clear the thought was on his mind, but Ripken wanted to handle the question in the way he tries to handle everything else—with style.

"I don't know. I think about it," Ripken said. "It floats in my head every once in a while because actually I'm asked so many questions. But the way that I cope with it, the way that I deal with it, is not to try to get ahead of myself. I say, 'OK, [I] can't do anything till it happens. ... I'll react to it then.' ... I don't like to anticipate, I don't like to think ahead, I don't like to get ahead of myself in that regard. It's a wonderful thought. You keep your fingers crossed that everything works out right, and I know it's going to be a flurry of emotions because I've gone through it with Eddie [Murray] when Eddie was inducted into the Hall of Fame ... I went up and watched the induction ceremony and Eddie took us all down a very emotional road, because you replay all the people that are important in your [life] and he focused on my dad. He looked at me and started talking about the importance of Dad to him and it made me cry. So, I mean, I know it's a wonderful emotional event; it's very special. It's the history of baseball celebrated and the game's best players, and the history of baseball is about people, and so to be included in the thought process and hopefully to be included in the Hall, it will be a wonderful thing. But I'm reserving my feelings for if and when this happens."

Entering The Hall

The 2007 induction ceremonies have received a lot of attention from the baseball world ever since people realized that Ripken and Tony Gwynn could be entering at the same time. An article on the MLB.com website in September 2006 painted an interesting picture of how difficult it might be for those visiting Cooperstown to actually find a place to stay within 100 miles of the small New York town that weekend. The combination of two players as well liked as Ripken and Gwynn could make for a very busy weekend. According to the MLB.com article, "Cooperstown and Hall officials are already bracing themselves for what they believe may be the largest induction turnout in history."

Polly Renckens, who's lived in Cooperstown nearly 40 years and served as president of the Chamber of Commerce, said in the article that Oriole fans have long been waiting for the day when Ripken makes the Hall of Fame.

"Let's put it this way," Renckens said. "We started getting calls about the 2007 Hall of Fame induction the day Cal Ripken announced that he was retiring after the 2001 season."

It will be a very interesting day for Baltimore fans and those who have been associated with the Orioles over a long period of time. They understand that Ripken is simply doing what he does now not only because he just loves the game, but also as a tribute to his father, a man who meant so much to so many people but never really got the credit he deserved. Ripken's induction into the Hall of Fame would be a nice honor for his father, who sadly isn't around anymore to see it.

Many big-time athletes in this day and age focus on two things, money and themselves. But, although his baseball projects gain revenue, Ripken is truly giving back to his home area. This is the main reason why Cooperstown could be overloaded with people dressed in orange and black when Ripken makes it into the Hall of Fame in the summer of 2007. The major question will be what kind of speech he'll give, and how he'll pay tribute to his father. Will the whole speech be

Baseball's Iron Man: Cal Ripken Jr., A Tribute

Although he has yet to enter the Hall of Fame, Ripken has always been in baseball's spotlight. *(Photo by Vincent Laforet/Getty Images)*

a tribute to his dad? Or, more than likely, will Ripken thank his father and credit the many people who helped in his career? Either way, it's a fair bet that Ripken is going to talk for a long time about his family and close friends in the sport.

It's likely to be an emotional day for many reasons. Ripken truly is the last really popular Oriole. At this time, players like Brian Roberts, Miguel Tejada, and Melvin Mora are growing in popularity, but nobody's come close to Ripken or some of the team's superstars from the days when any American League team had to get past the Orioles to do something worthy. The Orioles now have had nine straight losing seasons, attendance is down, and players don't have the popularity they did before. But Ripken still does.

Late last season, the Detroit Tigers came to Oriole Park with about a week left in the season, fighting to hold onto first place in the

Central Division and make the playoffs. Manager Jim Leyland talked to the media before the afternoon game and discussed how his team had surprised him. Then he paused.

"Has Cal been here?" he asked, wondering how often Ripken had come to Oriole Park. Leyland then talked about how much he admired Ripken. The skipper had gone to some of Ripken's fantasy camps, and spoke for several minutes about how much he loved to see what Ripken was doing in terms of building a new ballpark and helping the game of baseball become even more popular for kids.

"He's doing some good stuff," Leyland said, nodding his head.

That's one reason why Ripken's entrance into the Hall of Fame will be so popular—and not just in Baltimore. He's touched so many people in so many ways all around the country and the world. Say the name "Cal" and most people know the discussion is about Ripken. That's what should keep his success going after the Hall of Fame ceremonies end.

But Ripken will continue in other directions even after the Hall of Fame. He'll carry on his work with minor league teams, and has made it clear that even if he makes the Hall of Fame, he'll still do his job in the same manner. Ripken handles things for his present teams, Aberdeen and Augusta, in a low-key way, mainly to make sure that everything keeps moving along.

"Even in the early stages ... looking at it from a big-picture standpoint, maybe it's more about getting [these public and private partnerships] started and getting [them] on the map," Ripken said. "I really believe in hiring the right people. Our group here is tremendous. We train other people ... so they can assume the responsibility in the next job. And so I'm a firm believer in letting them do their work. I know I'm a promotional tool of sorts. If there's a bump in the road that I might need to go down there and help out, I can. I'm curious to see how things go. I like to look at designs and how we can improve things from time to time. I'm happy to say, in some ways, the

IronBirds don't need me around here. The community has grabbed a hold of this place in an unbelievable way. I like to come in here to eat crabs, to watch a game periodically, but by no means do I need to be here for the success of the business. It does a great job on its own. My role is to get it started."

And he's certainly done that.

20

IN THE END...

In the end, Ripken's story is truly an old-fashioned one. It's about a local boy who makes good—very, very good—while playing for his hometown team. And he's done even more afterward. Ripken always had a hope and a vision for what his career would become—it would involve baseball, of course—and he was fortunate to have it all work out nicely.

At the press conference where he announced his retirement, Ripken even addressed this in a very succinct yet grateful manner.

"Well, I think I've said a lot thinking about my own playing career. If you were to set out to try to write a story about an ideal situation or an ideal career for a baseball player, I think my story would have to be considered," Ripken said. "I'm a hometown guy, my dad was with the Orioles, I can't tell you when the Orioles [weren't] really, really important to me, because I can't remember that far back. As far back as my memory will allow me, baseball and the Orioles were it ... and then I was able to be drafted against all odds, against big odds, with the Orioles, then make it in the Orioles and then actually have a long career with the Orioles. If you just add up all the odds against that sort of thing happening, it's pretty remarkable, and along the way there were many, many other good things that happened besides the ones I mentioned. But I feel lucky."

His luck continued after retirement, when he bought and placed a minor-league team—affiliated with the Orioles—right by his hometown. So many people love the fact that Ripken has actually come back to the area he came from. They take pride that they knew him then and know him now.

Go to anyone from Harford County, and it won't be hard to find some kind of connection to Ripken. They knew one of his siblings, dealt with his dad, or played with this one or that one. The Ripkens are kind of like sports royalty in the area, and you won't hear many bad opinions of them.

Joe Stetka played for Bel Air in the late '70s while Ripken was on the Aberdeen High team. Stetka remembers Ripken as small and thin—as many others can confirm—and he loves to kid Cal now that all of those milk commercials paid off nicely.

"There's no air with him at all," Stetka said. "What you see is what you get. Sr. and his mom [Vi] had a lot to do with that."

Stetka also speaks for many when he talks with pride about the type of player Ripken grew into.

"He played the game the way the game was supposed to be played," Stetka said. "When the game was over, that was it. He wasn't a troublemaker. He loved the game of baseball, and that was his mission. He played hard 162 games a year. To me, he's a great example for kids about just the way the game's to be played. Nobody played any harder than he did. He stuck it out and played. … The guy just flat out gave everything he had. I never saw him dog a ball, and I watched a lot of baseball. The guy is the true meaning of how baseball is supposed to be played. Billy, his brother, nobody played the game harder than he did also. I think his dad had a ton of influence as well, and that's a good thing."

In The End...

Many people who knew Jr. in Harford County also have plenty of good things to say about his father. So many people knew him in so many ways. Cal Sr. was a legend in the area before his son even made it to the Orioles, which helps the legend of his son grow even larger.

"I would talk to him occasionally about situations because I knew him through knowing Cal," Stetka said. "I've been coaching baseball for 14 years at the high school and recreation level, and I sit and watch the games, and I'll learn something. Sr. always had the positive things. He had a booklet he used for his workouts. You coach old school, like I do, and it's fundamentals, fundamentals, fundamentals. That's what Sr. preached and banged into people's heads. The balls always have been round, and the bats have always been round. I coach today solely on fundamentals. Cal Ripken Sr., Cal Ripken Jr., Billy Ripken, and fundamentals, that's the old school; that's the way the game was meant to be taught. That's the way it should be. I had a good teacher in his father. I would see him throughout the county and at other games and I would just talk to him. The guy, he was just fun to talk to because he just knew the game so well that anything you asked him, he knew the answer to. And I think a lot of Sr. I see in Jr., absolutely. It's just the way he plays the game."

When asked what he saw for Ripken in the future, Stetka said he'd probably keep doing what he's been doing for years. Along with his brother, he puts on clinics and gives back to his community. Stetka, in addition to serving as the assistant varsity coach at C.M. Wright High, is president of Hickory Fountain Green baseball, as well as a Cal Ripken Baseball commissioner for District 13. He's also the IronBirds' official scorer.

"Hey, I even pull the tarp, and I'm 49," he said with a laugh.

There's no question that Ripken could have made other plans for the IronBirds. Simply put, he could have placed that team anywhere in the United States. But he chose to come back home, and it's been a big plus for the area. As Melewski said, the Ripken influence is huge.

Baseball's Iron Man: Cal Ripken Jr., A Tribute

"I travel around the New York-Penn League in the minors, and the [IronBirds] are the envy of most minor league franchises because of how [they're] run," Melewski said. "We have more employees, we have a better stadium, we have a classier presentation, we have more scoreboards, we have more audio-video, we just have everything over most teams because of who Cal is. Cal attracts sponsors, Cal attracts fans, Cal attracts everything. His name on that franchise means everything. If it [were] Player X who was a marginal major leaguer who [owned] the IronBirds, in my opinion, they wouldn't be nearly as successful.

"He's also doing what his dad did, which was teach baseball at the youth level, teach it the right way, spread the word. It's amazing what he's doing. He and Bill love the game, they love to teach it whether there's two kids, whether there's 200 or 2,000, and they do what their dad taught them, which is to play the game the Oriole Way. You know, when Cal Sr. died, a little bit of the Oriole Way went with him, because he was the Oriole Way."

Cal Ripken Jr. grew into the personification of the Oriole Way during his career. And as time went on and the Orioles slid into trouble, Ripken represented to many some of the last vestiges of a magical time. The Oriole Way was the way everyone wanted to emulate because the team kept winning for nearly 20 years. But when the times began to change, there was no question that people would miss him, probably more so because he meant so much to so many as the hometown boy who made good.

Jeff Conine told reporters this on the day of Ripken's final game, and his message spoke volumes.

"It's going to be strange without him here next year," Conine said. "You know, you think of the Orioles and you think of Cal and Camden Yards and you realize that he is a fixture of this organization. I've only been here three years, but in my time here I have noticed how

Children are taught "The Ripken Way" at the Myrtle Beach complex.
(Photo by Business Wire via Getty Images)

much he means to this team and this city, and so it will be strange to not have him around next season."

Ripken talked at his retirement press conference about what pushed him to give so much so often. Was he the most talented shortstop or third baseman? No, he was not. But nobody outworked him. He talked about past conversations with teammates who were retiring and why some of them had regrets when it was over.

"From the very early point in my career, I was around players that were ready for retirement," Ripken said that day. "I remember I had a curiosity. In the back of the bus, I'd ask them questions like 'Now that you're at this point in your career, do you have any regrets looking back over your career?' More times than not, I'd hear responses like, 'I wish I would have taken care of myself better, I wish I would have played more, I wish I'd have taken it more seriously.' Those are the kind of comments I got when I was polling these players. Maybe that was the motivation for wanting to try to maximize and doing everything I can and maybe that was some of the motivation for showing up and playing every single day. I didn't want to be in a position at the end of my career to look back over it and regret not going about it a certain way. When I look back on my career, I had a certain set of skills, and I tried to maximize that. I tried to maximize my playing opportunity, and I tried to love every minute I was on the field. So when I look back on my career, I don't have those sort of regrets. I accomplished what my skills ... and my ability and my determination allowed me to."

People in Harford County and Baltimore still talk about those characteristics. There was nothing complicated about Ripken. He truly was a blue-collar guy from a blue-collar town, and a person so many people could identify with for so many reasons. He would stop and sign autographs for everyone. He would stop and talk baseball with nearly anyone. His father had been well known for similar reasons, and his son's life was about baseball. And now, as he prepares to go into the Hall of Fame, it's just another reason for Baltimoreans to take pride in Cal. The modern-day generation's Brooks Robinson, Ripken means so much to so many and his legend will only grow as his baseball programs grow. Because in the end, Cal Ripken Jr. is doing

In The End...

only one thing—exactly what his father loved to do—and he's doing it in the place he was born.

INDEX

Index

Index

Celebrate the Heroes of Maryland Sports
in These Other Releases from Sports Publishing!

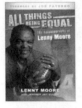